No, Minister!

Professor E. C. Wragg
Exeter University

Trentham Books

First published in 1993 by Trentham Books Limited

Trentham Books Limited
Westview House
734 London Road
Oakhill
Stoke-on-Trent
Staffordshire
England ST4 5NP

British Library Cataloguing Publication Data
A catalogue record for this book is available from the British Library.

ISBN: 1 85856 006 3

Designed and typeset by Trentham Print Design Limited, Chester
and printed by Bemrose Shafron Limited, Chester

Contents

Foreword   v

Chapter 1: No, Minister!

Sad to see an old friend in trouble   1
Gouda man slams in the lamb   4
Smile, it's election year   7
Ton-up Clarkie leaves the rest gasping   10
Peace, partnership and flying pigs   13
Vlad tidings for the major school market   16
Descartes thinks but Clarke Disney   19
He came, he saw, he blundered   22
Rubbish from the White Paper basket   25
Major drama looms out of mere crisis   28
Splitting hairs about split infinitives   31
Erasmus performs to get his goat   34
What a load of spherical objects!   37
I am not a free man, I am a number   40
Ted's guide to festive frolics   43
Beware Horace, sound-bite trendy   46
Wimps who think they are Tarzan   49
Petrified by prehistoric methods   52

Chapter 2: Mad Curriculum Disease

Follies that confound the SATirists   55
Don't shoot, I'm only the SAT tracker   58
Hide under the table and plead sanity   61
Bad language and the wages of syntax   64
Government anthology key stage 3   67
Ruled by the free market Stalinists   70
Must Paul be written off?   73
Don't put a moral lead on our necks   76
The sooner you spot where he's falling down
the sooner you can lend a hand   79
Exclusive — those tests in full   81
There's no knowing where we're going   84
Peace in the civil English war   87
Flying a kite for future technologists   91
Stop the mad whirligig, I want to get off   93
Give the GCSE more of a chance   95
The fire is out but who will clear up the mess?   97

Chapter 3: Life in the Classroom

Class conscious? 101
Headless chickens fricasseed 105
And for our top scorers, a gilt-edged P45 108
The tell-tale traits of a primary staffer 111
The Plowden Retort 114
Light shed on leading questions 117
Ain't misbehavin' 119
Shout and be damned 122
The shock of the new 125
The most delicate balancing act 127
A five-day week in the lions' den 129
The waiting game that brings rich rewards 132
Bugs ironed out of explanations 134

Chapter 4: Management Blues

Selling Swinesville with porky pies 137
Let's have a big hand for the chief chimp 140
Feeling a pang of inspector remorse 143
In a right-wing land, Arbut is king 146
An easy scapegoat for Clarke's propaganda 149
Nightmare on LMS street 152
Trust me, I'm a certified plonker 155
Forward to the bad old days 158
That crazy circular in full... 161
School children need testing 164
What they did in our holidays 166
Doctor, doctor, how my brain hurts 169
Recycling the bumf they peddle 172
How to win funds and influence people 175
New inspectors ancient and modern 178
The polys are sitting pretty 181
Seeds of destruction being sown in a three-class system 184
No solution to the sum of discontent 187

Foreword

'How do you think them up — you know, the columns you write for the Times Educational Supplement?' I am sometimes asked. No problem, I explain. I am harmlessly walking along, whistling a happy tune, when some idiot hurls himself across the path bearing an official document on some ministerial statement about testing pupils or the national curriculum. It is not so much satire, more a matter of copying bits out.

Sometimes I write a piece so exaggerated, so over the top, I wonder if my friends will think I have finally flipped. A week later I open a newspaper, or switch on radio or television, and find that my mad flight of fantasy is, if anything, an understatement of what is actually happening.

With so many changes of policy (on one occasion we received a letter approving our articled teacher course from the same government department which had written to us the previous week announcing the ending of the same scheme), the constant rubbishing of teachers and anyone who works in education, and a nostalgia for the nineteenth century that would not be shared by anyone who knew what actually happened in education during that period, it is a question of whether to laugh or cry.

I prefer to laugh, while at the same time getting on with the serious business of trying to make education work for millions of youngsters who gain little from political machinations, but a great deal from their teachers. Having a good laugh about the sheer daftness of some of the things they are asked to do has saved many a teacher from deep depression. The teaching profession is much more highly esteemed in many other countries than it is here.

I have no doubt that, in the 21st century, there will be widespread condemnation of the ham-fisted way in which the governments of the late 1980s and early 1990s tried to bury schools under a welter of detailed prescription that would have outraged R A Butler. Governments should stick to broad policy issues and not try to run schools from the centre. If they do they become ineffective and comical.

This is the sixth collection of my articles to be published by Trentham Books. It covers the period September 1991 to August 1993, a time when ministerial initiatives reached even more lyrical heights of lunacy. I wonder if they have yet peaked.

Ted Wragg

Chapter 1

No, Minister!

Sad to see an old friend in trouble

A lot of newsworthy events happened during the summer, so I thought I would recap the main stories in case you missed them. The big one, as they say, was that sensational coup. One minute things were running normally, the next there was a take-over by the hard-liners. Yes, I was as surprised as anyone about the changes at the School Examinations and Assessment Council.

Another was the sad news that an old friend of yours and mine had run into a spot of bother. I stumbled across this one in rather a strange manner when I happened to be passing the front of a town-centre bookshop. Set in the middle of a large window display was a placard advertising a book called, believe it or not, *Where is Wally now?* Apparently, so the ad proclaimed, there is a whole set of books known as the Wally series of which the best known, though I had never heard of it, was *Where is Wally?* The latest gripping title in the series is *Where is Wally now?*

I would have remained mystified by this intriguing question had I not glimpsed a newspaper vendor's placard, right next to the bookshop, which read *Baker under fire*, and which answered it immediately. The lead story was about Kenneth Baker and his problems at the Home Office over escaping prisoners and numerous other matters. Trouble seems to follow the man around. Cometh the hour, cometh the Wally.

As I read the main story my heart sank. The phrases in it were chilling — 'They will have to be licensed or put down'. The awful thought entered my mind that Wally must have been put back in charge of the Department of Education and Science. He did like the licensed teacher scheme, but wasn't this going too far? It got worse — 'They will have to be muzzled in public', 'must be kept on lead at all times', 'grave threat to people's safety', and, getting serious now, 'neutered by Christmas'.

Steady on, old chap, I know you were not too fond of teachers, but isn't all this a bit over the top? Fortunately the story was about pit bull terriers and the Dangerous Dogs Act, to my immense relief. You can get back your negotiating rights if someone takes them away, but, unless there is some miracle of surgery that has escaped my notice, the same cannot be said about your goolies.

Next there was John Major's Citizen's Charter, promising everything the consumer could ever desire, including the removal of motorway cones and financial compensation if your train is late, the latter a nice thought, but then there would be even less money available to buy new trains that won't break down in the first place. It looked to be another variant on the ancient theme, 'Paradise is just a general election away'.

What worried me was the assumption that public servants are there to be fined, pilloried and vilified if things go wrong. This is fair enough, maybe, if they were acting incompetently or with malice, but if someone does badly at school it is wrong to assume that this is as a result of professional incompetence when there might be a shortage of books, equipment, lack of parental support or, indeed, the pupil concerned may have made little effort.

The most chilling feature of the charter, however, was the victory for the hard-liners represented by the introduction of league tables of schools' raw unadjusted test scores. Although league tables had been talked about, it seemed unlikely that anyone, other than estate agents, would actually compile them, but they are in the charter.

In case you missed the detail, here is what is going to happen. Every school will be obliged by law to compile its national tests scores at 7, 11, 14 and 16 and send them to the Football League. The top 22 schools will then break away to form a Premier League, and the rest will be put into regional leagues sponsored by well-known firms, like the Doggifood Conference Division, the Fly-by-Night Intermediate League and the Arthur Daley 'Ere Want a Cheap Watch Guv Senior League.

Instead of the familiar format of 'played, won, lost, drawn . . ' the tables will be compiled under new categories. Take, for example, a league table of primary schools which have just completed the tests for seven-year-olds. A pupil who obtained level 3 in maths, science and English, will score one *Smartass*. Anyone who told all his friends he was going to get a row of 3s, but actually obtained all level 1s, scores one *Baker*. In the floating and sinking test, pupils who thought that a 50 ton lead weight would float, or who shoved the pineapple into their left ear instead of putting it in the water, will be a *Clarke*.

Anyone whose name escapes you will be recorded as a *Junior Minister*. If you cannot remember what exam grades pupils got, then put them down as a *Major*.

Finally all teachers will be given a two-day in-service training course, to introduce them to the new league table cliches, and help them learn how to explain to the public why Scumbag Primary School is bottom of the Failstart Lawnmower Division and has been relegated to the Rusti Garden Rakes League. 'Half-way through the teacher assessments, Brian, we was over the moon. The lads done great, and the lasses done even greater.'

'But it was a season of two halves. Everyone gave 200 per cent, and the staff would have gone through a brick wall for me. Some did. I can't talk about next week, Brian, we take one SAT at a time. You're only as good as your last SAT. We're gutted Brian, sick as a parrot, but we'll keep battling, take each SAT as it comes, and, come the end of the next SATs, we'll be there or thereabouts, Brian...'

Times Educational Supplement 6.9.91

Gouda man slams in the lamb

A butcher can inspect a school. Yes, it's official. Recently Kenneth Clarke was asked if, given that he thought anyone could inspect a school, a butcher might one day perform the honours. Our estimable Secretary of State duly confirmed that a butcher could indeed wield his chopper on the educational system. Her Majesty's Inspectorate is at this moment writing its latest masterpiece, *A Butcher's Guide to School Inspection*, published by HMSO at £29.95 (or loose, £9.95 a pound).

I look forward to the meat purveyor's perspective on such matters as whether or not the teacher is using a suitable language register, or giving appropriate practical experience, when explaining concepts to children with learning difficulties, or 'pupils at the scrag end of the educational system', as they will no doubt be known. I can hardly wait for a verdict on cross-curricular themes in the national curriculum, the very steak and kidney pie of primary education, or what to do with disruptive adolescents. Let us not mince words, sausages, it's absolutely offal. Veal hate it.

You may well wonder what on earth press conferences are like if you have only seen one on television. Kenneth Clarke tends to sit there like a big slab of Gouda, effortlessly churning out the clichés, confirming the Prime Minister's shrewd selection of him to bland for Britain in the forthcoming World Hackney Championships sponsored by Bromide. Since the Big Cheese is currently on a wheeze-a-week campaign in the run-up to an election, these platitude-laden press conferences seem to take place all the time, usually in front of the Department of Education and Science logo, under the slogan, 'If you're in a mess, phone the DES'. In case you missed the last one, here is a transcript.

'Ladies and gentlemen, welcome to my latest press conference in which I shall be announcing some important developments in primary education. First of all let me say something about the testing of seven-year-olds. You will note from the 600 page press release that I have changed some of the set books since last year. We have decided to drop *Little Twinky Smokes Pot* and replace it with *Little Twinky Becomes a Stockbroker*. Teachers will require children to read 100 words from a set text, and since it was pointed out last year that *Little Twinky Buys his Council Flat* was only 91 words long, I have instructed teachers to make them read the words inside the back cover as well: 'All rights reserved London and New York. Vote Conservative'.

'Next I want to tell you about the inquiry I am setting up into primary teaching. This will be a far-reaching study and will report next Tuesday. I have given the committee a free hand with no government interference, to find out why primary schools are such a shambles. Objective background information will be brought to the committee's attention to focus its thinking, like the excellent research conducted by Colonel Adam Smith-Rightwinger into primary teachers, *They're all Marxists, the bastards.*

'The brief includes fundamental, but open questions such as: 'Should children be streamed at birth?' and 'Why oh why is topic and project work such a waste of time, when we never did it at my public school and I can't say that's ever been a handicap to me?' There is the supplementary question the committee will address: 'Shall we make children sit in rows from January onwards, or will it take a few weeks longer to sell off all the tables and buy some decent desks?'

'I should like to deny most strenuously the accusation from my critics that I simply hanker after the past and wish to restore what went on in previous centuries. Verily that is most disagreeable. I hold ye teacher in ye highest regard, i' faith. To him who speaks ill of me I say, 'Hist, mongrel grim, thou know'st me not.' It would be rather nice to hear ye 12 times table being chanted again though. Now, any questions, varlets?'

'*Anne Scroggins, 'Daily Globe'. Mr Clarke, I have managed to obtain a copy of the letter you have written to the members of this primary inquiry committee, in which you say: 'I am writing to ask you to serve on a committee of inquiry into primary education. Please bring your own hatchet to the first meeting. PS: Really put the boot in, lads, or you'll all be singing soprano.' Would you like to comment on that?*'

'I repeat what I have already said. The committee will be entirely free to write its report in my own words. Next question.'

'*Bill Ponsonby, 'Sunday Bugle'. Mr Clarke, is it true that what you know about education could be written down on the back of a postage stamp and still leave enough room for a couple of verses of 'Rule Britannia'? And that you never answer journalists' questions properly because you are so ignorant about what is happening?*'

'Let me repeat what I have already said. Labour councils and the teacher unions have ruined primary schools. Yes, chap at the back in grey suit and glasses'.

John Major, 'Prime Minister's Gazette'. Mr Clarke, would you repeat after me the following words: 'I will do exactly what I am told if I want to stay in the Cabinet'?'

'I will do exactly what I am told if I want to stay in the Cabinet. Yes, next question, man at the back in the blue-and- white striped apron with the big basket.'

'Dewhurst, 'Butchers' Monthly'. Mr Clarke, I don't really understand any of this. Can you explain to me exactly what they do in primary schools?'

'Ah, can I have a couple of pork chops please, and some of that nice lamb? Would you mind inspecting a school for me before you go? You wouldn't like to be on my primary committee by any chance, would you? Don't forget to bring your cleaver.'

Times Educational Supplement 13.12.91

Smile, it's election year

Did you catch the predictions made by Ministers about what will happen in 1992? They were little belters. Writing in *The Times*, Kenneth Clarke was pictured over a caption which read: 'Teachers will he better paid and schools and pupils happier'. The article was full of nice observations like: 'Teachers will have become more relaxed about change and public accountability for their performance' and 'The education system will be coming to its senses'.

Don't you wish you had met Kenneth Clarke earlier in your career, so that you could have 'come to your senses' — sooner? Instead you wasted time trying to teach, when you could have been more usefully filling in all his forms and reading his daft documents. Never mind, you are going to be more relaxed and enjoy life more in 1992. The Minister says so. And if you don't, then he will introduce the 1992 Education Act to *make* you smile, whether you want to or not, as part of the Citizen's Charter.

The 1992 Education Act has been secretly drawn up in draft form, and the 'smile' clauses are already proving controversial. Clause 239 (b)(ii), for example, states: 'Teachers shall be required to smile at all times, even when kicked on the shin by disruptive pupils or visiting ministers, to say 'Have a nice day' when greeting each other, to wear a badge with the slogan 'I'm hap hap happy' and to laugh deliriously when studying their bank statement'. Smile-related pay is described in other clauses, and there will be **chuckle bonuses** available to those demonstrating most mirth.

Earning a **chuckle bonus** will be made easier if you read the rest of Clarkie's predictions, especially the one saying that 'schools will look brighter and better repaired'. Under clause 358 (c)(iii) of the 1992 Education Act, any school refusing to look brighter and better repaired after due warning will simply he blown up.

If you want to qualify for the really big smile-related pay increases, however, the brand new 1992 chortle increments and **mega-guffaw awards**, then turn to the other set of predictions for 1992 made in the Guardian by junior minister Michael Fallon. Big Mike came up with a really nifty wheeze when asked to pen some comments on the coming year, and decided to write a brisk little parody of schools and local education authorities by pretending they were shops and LSAs (local shopping authorities).

Now get ready to split your sides at all this. Big Mike described how shopping (schooling) would he put on a statutory basis, and local shopping authorities would not allow shopworkers to be reposted or dismissed in under two years because of 'staff protection'. Shoppers would have to use the one supermarket and one corner shop in each area. Are you sure you get all this, by the way, because it is pretty subtle? Any way the gist of the message was that it was very silly to blame the Government for anything that was wrong in education as it was really the fault of LEAs and schools as they now are, and what we all needed was a sensible bit of market economics.

I once played football with a lad who scored more own goals than anyone. He could slice clearances into his own net, tap a backpass beyond his own goalkeeper, head corners gently under his own crossbar better than anyone I had ever met until I encountered Big Mike. Whereas most own goals trickle over the line as a result of embarrassing accidents, Big Mike prefers to thunder them into the net from 40 yards out, leaving the goalkeeper and everyone else astounded.

When members of the Government start discussing their educational ideology, for want of a better word, you can guarantee that cans of beans will not be far behind. If you want to extend the schooling/shopping metaphor in terms of what we actually have now, rather than spoof predictions for 1992, then nothing could be easier. The 1988 Great Shopping Reform Act was introduced when Kenneth Baker was Minister of Shopping. This compelled all shops by law to offer exactly the same goods. Shops were sent over thirty booklets and ringbound folders of government regulations covering in minute detail exactly what could be sold. This was known as the National Shopping Catalogue. 'Independent shops' however, about 6 per cent of the total, were allowed to sell anything they wanted, without government interference.

'Independent shops' were also allowed to select their customers, usually the most wealthy and privileged, and had 50 to a 100 per cent more shop assistants than the other 94 per cent of 'maintained shops' as they were known, which had to serve every customer who came on to the premises. In the 1980 Shopping Act the government introduced an 'assisted purchases' scheme and actually paid millions of pounds of public money to customers as an inducement to use the 'independent shops'.

Furthermore the 'independent shops' were not subject to the annual test imposed on all the other shops by the Government. They were also excused from filling in all the government forms which prevented shop assistants in 'maintained shops' from spending their time serving customers properly. Ministers continued to pour scorn on shop assistants in ordinary shops, even though they were working in difficult circumstances.

The profits of 'maintained shops' were determined by a formula laid down by the government under a scheme known as 'local management' the 'localness' of which had most shop assistants in permanent hysterics. Meanwhile the government introduced a new type of semi-independent shop, the 'grant-maintained' and 'city technology' shops, which were promptly given millions of pounds of public money for new premises while ordinary shops had to make do with leaking roofs.

Control over shops, Mike? The Government has left everyone else standing. Shop assistants in ordinary shops do far more than just sell cans of beans. They might earn more **chuckle bonuses** in 1992 if there was fair competition, and the professionalism of what they did was genuinely appreciated, not just played with for election purposes.

Times Educational Supplement 10.1.92

Ton-up Clarkie leaves the rest gasping

It is a sign of the times, perhaps, that a great deal of press coverage has been devoted to a group of joyriders who operate at high speed, sometimes doing more than 100 miles per hour, performing regularly in front of crowds of admirers gathered to watch their hair-raising antics. There appears to be little the police can do about them, and some have become media characters, bragging to reporters that no one can stop them.

I refer, of course, to that band of ministers who spin off improbable yarns at such incredible velocity that few can catch up with them. Dubbed 'whoppers' by the newspapers, they tell their big ones at speeds way in excess of the national limits as they scorch round the estate where they live — 'The House' as it is known locally — astonishing members at their audacity. A man claiming to be their spokesman, known simply as 'Clarkie', boasted: 'They can't get near us. I often come up with something so daft I have to laugh myself, but by the time someone has spotted it I'm off the estate, doing a ton again.'

'Clarkie' has explained to the press some of the jargon that has grown up around this late-20th century phenomenon. The best known technique is 'ram raiding'.

This involves one minister telling a bit of a porky, and then another storming over the top with an absolute whopper. Clarkie often works as a twosome with his mate, nicknamed 'Egger', according to others on the estate, either because he eggs Clarkie on to higher speeds and more dangerous stunts, or because he overeggs the cake.

Vrooooom! 'There has been wide praise from teachers for the SATs... teacher friendly ...the broad lines are OK,' said Egger to the National Association of Head Teachers in June. Peeeeeeow! The only complaints came from a few dissidents in the National Union of Teachers, scorched Clarkie, hurling himself suicidally, Evel Knievel style, in his supercharged turbo, over the top of 20 London buses. Both usually wear ski masks — not that anyone has noticed.

Then there is the 'handbrake turn' — a dangerous manoeuvre that involves going at very high speed in one direction and suddenly applying the handbrake so you make a 180-degree turn into reverse. Zoooooom! There is no preferential financial treatment for grant-maintained schools when they opt out of local authority control, claimed Clarkie at the North of England Conference in January. Indeed it was extremely naughty to talk about 'bribery'.

But, a few months later — Screeeech! Look out! Here comes 'Major', the Mr Big of the whoppers, doing a sensational handbrake turn in a letter to the NUT last month: 'We have made no secret of the fact that grant-maintained schools get preferential treatment in allocating grants to capital expenditure. We look favourably at grant- maintained schools to encourage growth of the sector, and I am delighted to see numbers are continuing to grow rapidly.' My dictionary defines bribery as 'money offered to procure action or decision in favour of giver'. Spot on, squire.

Next there is the 'screamer'. This occurs when one of the whoppers hurtles through at such breathtaking velocity that he is out of sight before anyone can say, 'What the hell . . .' Again one of the top practitioners of this frenetic art is the ubiquitous Clarkie, who actually said at a press conference about the privatisation of the school inspection service: 'Anyone can inspect a school.' 'Would this include certified loonies, chimpanzees and Al Capone, one wanted to ask, but too late. A puff of cigar smoke, a faint whiff of draught lager, and Clarkie was light years away.

Occasionally whoppers will provide some comic relief for the spectators and send out 'Big Mike' Fallon in his baggy costume to ride round on a clapped-out motor scooter at about three miles an hour, sounding off about how *EastEnders* is ruining the nation's youth, clippety clop, clippety clop. It is a bit like Nigel Mansell and Ayrton Senna having a little race on kiddies' trikes — you know they can go at 200 miles per hour round Monza if they want to, but, good sports that they are, anything for a laugh.

One of the more impressive pieces of comic relief again came from Clarkie, in holiday mood. When asked why the Government was removing subsidies from non-vocational adult education, which would mean that fees would be trebled or quadrupled, and probably kill it off altogether for many people, he said that he did not see why public money should be spent subsidising evening classes for wealthy old-age pensioners in his constituency, which is a rather humorous view of a move that may well end adult and community education for hundreds of thousands of needy people. Clippety clop, clippety clop. Send in the clowns.

One of the most amazing techniques is the 'sound of silence'. Here the whoppers say nothing at all. Clarkie was again peerless when he appeared before a parliamentary select committee and claimed there was nothing he could do to improve standards of reading, as he was not really in charge. Yet he controls the curriculum, the testing, the cash, the salaries and conditions of teachers, was able to dispense with the heads of the National Curriculum Council and the School Examinations and Assessment Council at little notice, and acquired more than 400 extra powers under the 1988 Education Act.

There was no profound comment when it was revealed that a school had taken on an 18-year old lad as a teacher at £8,500 a year.

But the whoppers have been revving up for a couple of years, saying there is no teacher shortage (although still investing a couple of million pounds in a recruiting campaign for an apparently non-existent problem) and endorsing the shabby licensed teacher scheme. Roll up, roll up, only one year of higher education necessary. Roll up, roll up, no years at all. (My son has just finished his GCSEs. Any offers?)

There was no perceptible rush through the sound barrier on this one. Stand back and applaud the breathtaking audacity of it all.

Times Educational Supplement 20.9.91

Peace, partnership and flying pigs

Our local newspaper sent me a questionnaire a few weeks ago. One question read: 'What are your hopes and fears for 1992?' I replied: '1993', on the grounds that people say things will get worse, but the optimist in me believes they can only get better. The most appealing aspect of post-Maastricht Europe for me would be if they decreed that national curricula had to be contained within single pamphlets, rather than three bookcases, but maybe Britain has taken an opt-out clause on that one.

My real chief hope for 1992 is that more than a hint of humanity will return to what government bureaucracy has tended to turn into a series of mechanical transactions. Instead, we may get yet another Education Act. The 1992 Education Act will probably decree that teachers' nervous breakdowns will only be permitted between 3 and 4pm on Fridays. The right to collapse under the strain any day of the week is one of the best freedoms left to the profession.

When I once talked to a conference of heads I told them a clinical psychologist I know had said she was treating more heads and teachers than ever for stress-related alcoholism. Many went on a regular weekend bender. 'Only at weekends then?' one head observed.

I suspect the passing of 1991 will be little mourned. It was another triumph for systems over the individual. In my research I often have to process large amounts of data. There comes that frustrating moment when you have used every multivariate statistical technique and still cannot see a pattern in the wretched mass of figures swimming before your eyes. It is tempting to programme into the suite of refined procedures the Utopia Option, an omni-purpose neat set of figures dreamed up in advance, which simply prints out when you press the right button. It would be useful to have the Utopia Option ready whenever systems threaten to take you over.

Some people fight back against the dreary bureaucracy of it all by lobbing in the word 'quality' at every turn. My own experiences of this brave attempt to humanise the inhuman have been somewhat negative. Whenever I have come across the Head of Absolutely Spiffing Quality in the Quality Assurance section of Little Piddlington Quality (Honest guv) Quality All the Way College, the titles have been papering over rubbish. Real quality needs no label. I do not recall seeing the tag 'top quality' on a Rembrandt masterpiece.

Deciding the Quality Awards for 1991 is no problem. Top quality 'Sorry if I've embarrassed you' award went to John Major, who said the exact opposite of what Kenneth Clarke had proclaimed in his speech at the beginning of the year to the North of England Conference. In the summer he wrote a letter to the National Union of Teachers which confirmed that grant maintained schools were indeed being bribed to opt out through large grants for new buildings.

Quality assurance move of the year was the Government's proposal to open up school inspection to psychopaths, spivs and anyone else capable of reading the two page 'How to Inspect a School' pamphlet being written at this very moment by Her Majesty's Inspectorate.

Best quality laugh came a few weeks ago. I was quietly watching the television news when suddenly this tremendous noise split the heavens from Land's End to John O'Groats. It was an enormous guffaw of delight emanating from the throats of hundreds of thousands of teachers across the entire nation. After all these years their belief in Santa Claus had at last been restored. They had just heard that Kenneth Baker had been done for contempt of court.

Ever since I discovered that Baker used to work for a tailoring firm I have wished be had stayed there. 'A little tight on the shoulders, sir?' It was just right.

Quality impression of the year was the one made by Kenneth Clarke on a group of teacher trainees. In an extremely rare visit to a teacher training course he sat in with a group of students discussing the run-up to the national curriculum in English. Eventually he interrupted to ask them what this Kingman Report was that they kept mentioning. The students sat in disbelief as the Minister had to have explained to him what a seminal report, commissioned by his own government on a core subject in the nation curriculum, was.

My real quality prize for 1991, however, was easy to decide. In October I shared a platform with Lord Callaghan and John MacGregor at Swansea University, celebrating the 15th anniversary of Jim Callaghan's Ruskin College lecture, which was delivered in 1976. Both made excellent speeches, but what was most impressive was that here were two politicians from different parties who really cared about education. It was such a refreshing change from the regular slagging of teachers and schools we have begun to take for granted.

If 1992 is to be more hopeful than 1991, I should like to see a different word in vogue again — 'partnership'. There was a time when schools, local authorities and government were all supposed to work together. Not that they always did, but at least there was a feeling that we were all supposed to be on the same side.

When Sir Edward Boyle set up the Plowden Committee in 1963 his successor, Anthony Crosland, simply took on board the report three years later. It is illustrative of the 1990s that the same report is being used as a political weapon, and Lady Plowden, this benign grandmother figure, is being cast as an unlikely villain in a silly political squabble. What a pleasure it would be if the future held a vision not of strife and contempt for those who work in education, but of harmonious collaboration for the common good. I also believe pigs can fly. Happy New Year.

Times Educational Supplement 27.12.91

ARE YOU THE TEACHER WHO WROTE IN TO COMPLAIN ABOUT WORKLOAD?

Vlad tidings for the Major school market

I'm getting a bit worried about the Prime Minister. 'Now don't you go attacking that nice Mr Major,' my mum is going to say, but that is just the trouble. He seems a decent chap, smiles a lot, likes football and cricket, tucks his shirt neatly into his underpants, dines at the Happy Eater, just the sort of bloke I'd like to be when I grow up. But he has now taken over the running of education, and that is what bothers me.

Look at the evidence. He said that education was his big idea, that teachers should have a decent car, so no more N-registered Minis bought with the Houghton Award in the mid-1970s. So far, so good. But then the signals began to be a little clearer.

When he made a speech on education, the audience he chose was the Centre for Policy Studies, the right-wing pressure group set up by Margaret Thatcher and Lord Joseph. Instead of visiting a primary and secondary school, he went on the morning and afternoon of his speech to a city technology college and a grant-maintained school.

Since then he has been closely involved in the removal of the heads of the two major advisory bodies, the National Curriculum Council and the School Examinations and Assessment Council, and their replacement by two former advisers to the Number 10 Policy Unit one of whom has blamed schools for the urban riots. He decreed league tables of schools' test scores, and initiated the sudden and unexpected massacre of Her Majesty's Inspectorate put out to private companies after 152 years of service.

I recently asked a senior person at the Department of Education and Science about a policy matter. Don't even ask, was the reply, as people at the DES hadn't a clue. Everything was being run from Number 10. They had not even seen the Prime Minister's speech. It was Major who was being briefed by the National Foundation for Educational Research on issues like testing seven-year-olds nowadays. Their minister seemed to have rolled over (distant rumbling sound of large falling body). Clarkeberg was probably the flattest lager in the world.

16

R A Butler often stated that politicians should keep some distance between themselves and classroom practice, otherwise schools would be at the mercy of individual whim. What concerns me about John Major is that most of what he has done so far represents a very strong move to the right, as the loony tunes of the market-mad right-wing pressure groups become reality. I had not thought he was that suggestible.

The right-wing groups and individuals, as revealed in their pamphlets and speeches, hate Her Majesty's Inspectorate and its independence, believe that teachers are dangerous trendies who need tight control, that teacher trainers are Marxists, that notions like 'equal opportunities' and 'special educational needs' are the whims of educationists (they are government policy, but never mind), that education is a production line with children instead of canned beans, hence their references to the efficiency of Tesco and Sainsbury and that less money should be spent on education, for which parents should pay more.

The Right believes that anyone can teach, a bit of subject knowledge being the sole requirement, so teacher training is no big deal as there is nothing to learn. Anyone can inspect a school, and the market controls quality, so 26,000 schools must be made into businesses, each in cut-throat competition with the others, with the least successful going bust, hence the league tables.

Educational thinking is no longer informed by advice from HMI, based on careful inspection of thousands of classrooms, but is instead prisoner to the ill-informed prejudices of right-wing ideologies, a chilling prospect.

Working on my 'leap-frog' theory of education (see which way things are moving, and then hop over the top and get there first), I have, therefore, decided to found an even more right-wing group, Vlad the Impaler Enterprises Inc. We at Vlad, under the trading slogan 'Go mad with Vlad', will be offering a fully comprehensive (oops, mustn't use that word), educational entrepreneurship in keeping with the national trend.

Our beans division offers a transfer system for pupils. We can sell you a pupil two national curriculum levels ahead of the norm for a couple of hundred in used notes, no VAT, no questions asked. For five hundred we will deliver to your door what we call our 'Gazza' model, someone three or more levels ahead.

Equally, the beans division will arrange to take off your hands, for a hundred a throw, any pupils who are not 'commercially attractive', for example, someone a level or two below average, or anyone who twitches a bit, smells, or otherwise puts off prospective affluent parents.

As you know the Government is keen to foster two-year degrees because they are cheaper. They are hoping that some of the dafter polytechnics will take up the idea, thereby consigning themselves to permanent second-class status and making us the laughing stock of Europe.

We at Vlad will go one better. Our higher education division offers a BA in two years, a BSA (Bachelor of Some Arts) in one year, and a BBA (Bachelor of Bugger All) in no years, for just a thousand in used tenners.

All BBA candidates who so wish can be licensed teachers. They will receive a free copy of my teacher training manual *Speak Up*, a concise one-page booklet consisting of just one sentence, 'Louder, you fool', the most cost-effective training course yet devised.

Our school inspection division will shortly be producing its prospectus. In true, learn-to shed tradition we shall offer several bespoke models. The *Whitewash*, which leaves you smelling sweeter than violets, will cost £10,000. The *Pasting* is on special offer to governing bodies who want their school doing over, at a mere £12,000. The obverse, for a bargain £15,000, aimed at the head who wants a searing critique of the chairman of governors, is our *Take That You Prat*.

Pick of the Vlad catalogue, a snip at £1,000,000, a triumph for the market, specially designed for those who want to restore the early 19th century in its entirety, is our *Major*. I just hope nobody buys it.

Times Educational Supplement 18.10.91

Descartes thinks but Clarke Disney

The news that several teachers had applied for jobs with Euro-Disney in France was depressing, especially when some said they did not care what job they took so long as they could escape, but it did not surprise me. It was probably the best chance they would ever get to present Mickey Mouse with a Kenneth Clarke watch — no hands, just two fingers pointing at the nearest school. Imagine arriving in Paris and finding that Clarkie and Michael Fallon had landed the plum jobs as Donald Duck and Goofy.

I nearly joined them myself when I read that Kenneth Clarke had been described by a colleague as 'one of the party's deeper thinkers'. *One of the party's deeper thinkers?* We are talking huge national emergencies here. Dial 999 immediately. Ask for the whole lot — police, ambulance, fire brigade, 7th Tank Regiment. If Clarkie is the party's Plato, then please, Euro-Disney, hire me immediately as a chipmunk, Snow White, anything, before I meet the party's Pluto.

Take the national curriculum, for example, What is desperately needed here is partly better thinking, partly better management. Anyone with more than 10 brain cells, Plato or Pluto, can see that it has become exactly what was predicted: a nightmare of 10 discrete, overly prescriptive, separately conceived subjects, rather than an intelligent framework for an organic whole curriculum. A real thinker and manager would find a way of making the enterprise simpler, clearer, challenging, but feasible.

Back in late July 1987, when Kenneth Baker began a lengthy consultation process that was to last well into the following week, some 11,790 people wrote in to offer their comments on the proposed national curriculum. Many were in favour of a central core, but, according to Julian Haviland, who read all the replies and then summarised them in his book *Take Care Mr Baker!*, precisely 11,790 out of 11,790 were against what was being proposed. This must still be the British, Commonwealth, European, World and Inter-galactic record for fore-warning.

Unfortunately Kenneth Baker, star of the Hollywood blockbuster *Jungle Macho Guy* ('Me future leader [pounds chest], me plough on to end of furrow, me no deviate under any circumstances from crappy plan') ignored all the unambiguous advice about the folly of locking 10 different groups of subject enthusiasts in 10 different rooms for several weeks. Every one else knew that what they collectively produced would not cohere and would probably add up to at least 200 per cent of the week.

In theory there was a way out, as the National Curriculum Council would later make sense of disparate and possibly self-contradictory proposals. Had John MacGregor, the only real ministerial thinker and manager in recent years, stayed at the DES, this two-tier strategy would have worked. Unfortunately the next Hollywood blockbuster saw the screen debut of Kenneth Clarke in *Jungle Macho Guy 2* ('Me future leader [tries to pound chest, has difficulty finding it, eventually swings fist, but misses], me plough on to end of six-pack, me deep-thinking Greek philosopher Pluto'), and the whole Silly Symphony then became political, more about power and control than sense.

The problem is that the first sifting of national curriculum documents was usually done by right-wing pressure groups, whose pronouncements were given more prominence in the press, and taken much more seriously by ministers, than the original reports. So English was supposed to have no grammar or structure, history no facts, and music was all reggae and no Mozart. The truth of the matter is that Brian Cox, chairman of the English working party, has had to write his own book to put the record straight (*Cox on Cox*, a very good, if disturbing, read), and the history syllabus is dripping with knowledge spread over five millennia. Many of our best classical musicians wrote to John Major saying they *liked* the music report and did not want children spending half their time learning how to spell Beethoven, instead of composing and performing.

Were Kenneth Clarke really a good thinker and manager, he would now get the national curriculum reduced to a single pamphlet, as in most other countries, introduce some flexibility and imagination, and abandon the empty rhetoric about teachers being trendy progressives who do not believe that children should know anything. Instead he neither thinks nor manages. His 'thinking' is confined to stating the blindingly obvious, like saying that trainee teachers should be able to control a class, as if no one had ever thought of it before. Not exactly Immanuel Kant.

His 'management' consists of flooding schools with more and more changes, and then having the cheek to berate teachers, in a television interview, for being unwilling to face up to change, as if there were only one or two minor amendments to cope with.

It is customary to say that people with Clarkie's penchant for management could not manage a whelk stall. But have you ever wondered what would happen if he really did apply the management philosophy he employs with teachers and the national curriculum to the proverbial whelk stall?

Just imagine you are working behind the counter of the great thinker's whelk stall, 'Arry Stottle's Mucho Macho Whelk Emporium'. The first thing he would do is deliver 20 tons of whelks. Before you had time to unpack them, 50 tons of mussels, 60 tons of periwinkles and 70 tons of cockles would arrive. By now up to your ears in marine gastropods, you would just be able to see 100 pantechnicons pulling in to drop off loads of cabbages, lettuce and tomatoes.

As you disappear from view, smothered, unable to find a single bloody whelk, let alone sell anybody one, consoled only by the thought that, with Baker and Clarke in charge, there will be no need to order oil and vinegar for the salad dressing, you are dimly aware of the great philosopher telling the press the usual Kant: it is all your fault and you will have to stop being a trendy whelk-seller. If Euro-Disney is looking for a really deep thinker to play the part of Dopey, then Kenneth Clarke, the Ludwig Wittgenstein of Westminster, must be their man.

Times Educational Supplement 7.2.92

He came, he saw, he blundered

Not one tear will be shed when Kenneth Clarke empties his desk at the Department of Education and Science for the last time next week. A few would flow if he returned, but even if the Conservatives are re-elected, he will be after some bigger role, Minister of Culture no doubt. I wonder what treasures he will load into his holdall as he departs. An unread copy of the Plowden Report? Dale Carnegie's less well known work *How to Lose Friends and Alienate People*? His *Thesaurus of Insults*?

When he first arrived at the DES someone said he was just the sort of bloke you might meet in a pub. You can meet some very rum coves in a pub and true enough, most of his thoughts on education did have a ring of the saloon bar of the *Dog and Duck*. 'A pie, a pint, and a platitude' was his motto, not really good enough for someone who, as they used to say before school reports became computerised, could do better.

Eighteen months ago, when he began his term of office, the conditions were very favourable for an incoming minister. The national curriculum could have been trimmed down to make it workable, bureaucracy was waiting to be reduced, and John MacGregor had swept up some of the odium left by Kenneth Baker. Anyone with energy, wit and good intentions might soon have been the most effective Secretary of State for decades. Instead Kenneth Clarke became master of the effortless cliché, was hissed at virtually every conference he addressed and teachers who were St Francis of Assisi lookalikes turned into foaming psychopaths at the mere mention of his name.

So where did he he go wrong? After all, he is clearly not stupid. A former barrister, who had specialised in representing some of the less well off, he should have brought intelligence and empathy to a brief like education. If nothing else the sight of junior minister Big Mike Fallon coming off the subs' bench to warm up should have concentrated his mind.

He promised to reduce bureaucracy, but actually increased it. A couple of weeks ago we received a letter from the DES telling us that he had approved our secondary articled teacher scheme. A week previously we had received another DES missive to say he had decided to end the scheme. In Clarkeland the bureaucracy goes backwards from death to birth, till everything meets at the same point in time and the Universe implodes, the exact opposite of the Big Bang — the Big Squish.

To understand what drove him it is essential to take into account the inescapable fact that he fancied himself as a future Prime Minister, what you might call the Curse of the Ken. Conservative supremos are elected not by the general party membership but by the MPs. This means that aspirant leaders see as their constituency their own mates in Parliament. They have to impress the liberal and reactionary wings of this disparate group. Both Kenneth Baker and Kenneth Clarke felt obliged to talk tough-sounding nonsense, about kicking sense into trendy teachers, in order to appease those who see such pointless thuggery as 'leadership'.

This involved over-simplification of the issues to the point of farce. Anyone disagreeing with him was labelled 'latter-day left-wing apostles of Plowden'. In this grotesquely simple world of stereotypes, teachers were naughty children, parents all agreed with every daft word he uttered, and trouble only occurred in Labour authorities, even though many dedicated Conservative councillors spoke angrily about the way the Government was treating schools and local education authorities.

What was more irritating was his cynical mis-statement of the true state of affairs. He gave the public the impression that a third of seven-year-olds could not read, when this was not the case. Yet here was the one person in the country who could have established exactly what the state of play was, since he had all the resources of the DES at his command.

His insistence that grant-maintained schools were not being offered bribes and his urging of delegates at the North of England Conference to get their bids in quickly if they believed bribes were on offer, won him no respect, especially when John Major later said: 'We have made no secret of the fact that grant-maintained schools get preferential treatment in allocating grants to capital expenditure'.

Now that he is about to go I shall commence work immediately on writing an account of the positive achievements of his 18-month ministry. It will be called *He Came, He Went* and it will be a very short book, well, just the covers and a photograph of him actually, to remind people of what he looked like. In fact, I've finished it already. This very slim work is being published in circular shape, so that it can be opened at his picture and stuck on the staffroom dart board.

I hope that when he finally leaves Sanctuary Buildings, the inappropriately named expensive new headquarters of the DES, unlamented, the deafening cheers of thousand of teachers echoing in his ears, he will quietly obey the instructions on top of his marmalade jar: 'Turn slowly and push off'. In the meantime, I am not often moved to verse, but I have spent several seconds composing this poem dedicated specially to his memory.

> So push off, Clarkie.
> You plumbed the shallows
> Of your mind
> A blokey bloke.
> 'Everything on one sheet of A4'
> Was your motto.
> Why didn't you read them?
>
> So just push off, Clarkie,
> Back to the *Dog and Duck*
> Where your thoughts were born.
> A pint, a cigar and a Big Mac.
> I shall miss you,
> Much as I would
> Toothache.

Times Educational Supplement 3.4.92

Rubbish from the White Paper basket

Apparently there is going to be yet another White Paper on education. The newspapers are full of speculation about what it will contain, ranging from predictions that it will herald an even bigger Education Bill than the 1988 Act, to my own suggestion that it will just be a single blank sheet of white paper with nothing on it, the ultimate minimalist White Paper, a little government joke to cheer up people who think that there is going to be yet more legislation.

If past form is anything to go by then it will be launched in the summer holidays with little time to reply. The lurid pink consultative paper on the national curriculum was produced in similar circumstances, late in July 1987 with replies by September, and that was the starting point for all the chaos that ensued. There was a one-liner on children with special needs, the technical and vocational initiative was equally invisible, and the whole thing was dripping with obvious pitfalls which have caused chaos ever since. Most of these could have been avoided with genuine consultation.

Fortunately someone has managed to rescue a screwed-up copy of a draft of the proposed White Paper from a waste bin at the newly renamed Department for Education (as opposed to the Department *against* Education presumably), so I am happy to be able to give you this world exclusive on what it will contain. It is very much in line with what has already been published about the Citizen's Charter.

Grant-maintained schools: Under the Government's plan to extend choice in education all schools will be forced to opt out. A section of the White Paper headed 'Compulsory choice' explains how schools will be completely free to choose between opting out and being closed down. Parents will be asked to vote in a ballot but there will always be a majority in favour, because those voting against opting out will be taken outside and shot. Private schools, however, may opt *in* though it is not yet clear what they would opt into, since there will be nothing left. The draft statement on how the two sectors will sail past each other like ships in the night reads as follows: 'You put your private school in, your state school out. Opt in, opt out, shake it all about. You do the Hokey Cokey and you turn around. That's what it's all about. Hey!' This is from the section headed 'Oh Hokey Cokey Cokey'.

The national curriculum: This is far too complex compared with what happens in other countries so it will be reduced in stages. The subjects will first be reduced from 10 to 2, 'Arts' and 'Sciences', and eventually to one, 'education'. There will be just one profile component, called 'Learning things', and one attainment target. 'Basic things to learn'. The 10 levels will be abolished and replaced by three new categories 'clever', 'average' and 'thick'. As part of the Parent's Charter all children will have their rating stamped on their forehead in indelible ink.

Examinations: The GCSE and A-level examination will be replaced by new examinations designed for the 21st century. These will be called the School Certificate and Higher School Certificate respectively. The coursework element will be progressively reduced and the examination element increased, until the written exam constitutes 98 per cent of the total in PE, 100 per cent in English, and 110 per cent in mathematics. There will be three written papers in PE. Paper 1 will be 'What game I would play if had any playing fields', Paper 2 'Armchair fitness: thinking about being active, a cost-effective cerebral approach to physical education', and Paper 3 'The history of cricket from W G Grace to that nice chap who opened for England after Geoff Boycott retired.'

Children with special needs: The existing categories and the term 'special needs' will be abolished and replaced by four new categories: 'idiot', 'bone idle', 'cripple', and 'keep this one out of your league table scores unless you want to be relegated to the Vauxhall Conference division'. Schools seeking to improve their league table-position will be able to transfer pupils in these categories to a new type of school known as 'dross academies'. This will ensure that all schools come joint top of their league tables, and that their local dross academy comes bottom.

Local authorities: These will be abolished and replaced by a National Schools Funding Council. The chairman will be Colonel Adam Smith-Rightwinger the famous Mafeking veteran, who is clinically dead, but will be allowed to do the job posthumously. County halls will be renamed bingo halls and become the venue for the regional draw in the national lottery. Private schools will be given £2,000 per pupil, city technology colleges and the schools that opted out first will be given whatever they ask for, and the remaining 24,999 schools that had to be forced to opt out will be awarded 50 free lottery tickets and take their chance. The word 'education' is to be deleted from all official documents and replaced by 'lucky dip'.

Parent's Charter: Teachers will have to wear name badges, but anyone writing 'Donald Duck', 'Gazza', 'Guess who?' or 'Kiss me quick' on the label will be made to remove motorway cones as part of the Citizen's Charter, unless this is their real name. At parents' evenings teachers will be required to wear motorway cones on their head, so that parents can recognise them.

The White Paper *'Anything for a Laugh. Ooh, missus. All right then, please yourself'* will be published on Sunday, August 9 at 2am. Replies must be sent tea-time August 10 at the latest to: Miss Kiss me quick, Room 101, Department for Lucky Dips, Frankie Howerd Memorial Unit, Sanctuary Buildings, Watford Gap service station.

Times Educational Supplement 12.6.92

Major drama looms out of mere crisis

Whenever the Prime Minister makes a speech about education he seems to choose his audience and location very carefully. His first significant statement was made to the Centre for Policy Studies; his most recent, in which he outlined his plan for what the press called a 'hit squad' of headteachers to take over failing inner-city schools, to an Adam Smith Institute celebration dinner. Why does he not give these keynote speeches to conferences of parent teacher associations, school governors, or teachers? Why does he feel the need to deliver them to right-wing pressure groups?

Perhaps he has to stay well in with those in the ascendancy in his party, or perhaps he is a very right-wing person who feels at home with the like-minded. Maybe he thinks they are all dotty and just need encouragement, which could be true, because they usually applaud what he says. Judging from his expressed views on education, he favours a return to the approaches that failed him so badly at school, so he goes and chats to the people most likely to welcome these. Apparently, the right-wing punters paid £100 a head for the dinner, so either it was a belting meal, or they are dafter than I thought.

The rest then falls into place: stereotype any problem as caused by trendy left-wing teachers and local authorities; apply a market solution, like sending in the liquidators, even if market forces have, to some extent, caused the difficulties; take a punitive line with those who may, for all one knows, be struggling bravely against the odds, and give them a public rubbishing. It is a million miles from the notion of educational and social priority schools endorsed by Labour and Conservative governments in the 1960s and 1970s. Then teachers in tough inner-city schools were seen as people society had a duty to support, if they were trying to do their jobs properly — not as the automatic scapegoats for whipped-up public wrath.

I wonder if John Major's audience, as they sipped their £20 consommé, munched their £40 sausage and mash, nibbled their £25 individual fruit tart, and washed it all down with their £15 worth of Tizer (musing perhaps that really smart free marketeers would have invested the hundred quid, read his speech in the newspapers the following morning, and dined at the local Spud U Like, listening to piped Mantovani) stopped to ask themselves a few questions about the nature of his master plan.

Why, for example, did Mr Major assume that inner-city schools were the ones that failed? How will government commissioners actually run schools? More intriguingly, how will this 'hit squad' of super headteachers move in and take over? Will their log book look something like this?

09.23: Tango Foxtrot, on patrol in Grimstown centre, receives mayday call from Gasworks county primary school. Chief inspector M'Choakumchild and super heads Gradgrind and Goering of the Greater Grimstown special patrol group switch on siren and drive specially equipped car to scene of incident. Reports of unruly Year 2 class.

09.27: Tango Foxtrot arrives at school. Year 2 pupils staging protest at having to do national tests in nine subjects. SH Gradgrind unloads emergency pack C, crawls towards location of incident and lobs 30 copies of Schonell simplified spelling test into room. No injuries sustained, except for sore index finger subsequently after marking them. Leave 09.57.

10.47: Disturbance reported by deputy head of Lower Grimstown sec mod. Angry parent remonstrating about lack of remedial teaching. Send radio emergency call to Delta minus, requesting chief inspector 'Greasy' Baker to be on standby with large amounts of soft soap.

12.24: Mayday call from head of Alderman Harry Ramsbottom comprehensive. Staff meeting in progress, some teachers refusing to do playground duty. Tango Foxtrot engages siren and SH Goering and Gradgrind don riot gear. Arrival at scene 12.29. Immediately NUT rep attacks SH Goering's right knee with groin, and AMMA rep launches savage assault on SH Gradgrind's fists with right eye. Order restored by 12.30. SH Goering takes over chairmanship of meeting. Any other business reached at 12.31. There being none, meeting closed.

14.12: Distress alarm sounded by deputy head of Inner Grimstown middle school. She reports that head is suffering bout of severe indecisiveness over how to assign incentive allowances. Arrive at scene 14.21. Chief inspector M'Choakumchild conducts formal examination of head and pronounces him terminally incompetent. Early retirement package agreed 14.25. Incentive allowances given to first two teachers in alphabet.

14.58: Alarm call received from Grimstown Community college. No money for books or equipment, roof leaking, toilets smelly, paint peeling, boiler broken, playground unsafe, no sports facilities, 15.12: SH Gradgrind distributes contents of inner city emergency pack B to staff, one copy each of government booklet, *Bluffing Your Way through the National Curriculum with no Resources*, Kenneth Clarke's helpful pamphlet, *Just Get on with Your Job, Suckers*, and the old DES paper, *A Framework for the Curriculum* (no reason for this last once but copies are taking up valuable space in the panda and could be worth £20 a skip when shredded). 15.47: Emergency call from head of Grimstown Academy for the Really Stupid. Someone has been sick on the stairs and caretaker is away. SH Gradgrind telephones Prime Minister for advice.

15.49: Head told to bog off and clean it up herself, as it serves her right for coming bottom of league table.

Times Educational Supplement 26.6.92

Splitting hairs about split infinitives

The other day I heard Kenneth Clarke split an infinitive. I know you are shocked but it is true, I swear. The man who said on one *Panorama* programme when talking about the teaching of English that if you made a grammatical error people would think you were stupid, did himself split an infinitive on another *Panorama* programme. I heard it with my own ears and there were gasps around the nation at this lapse by such a prominent defender of grammatical rectitude.

Clarkie is, of course, quite right about the effect of a grammatical error on the audience. When I heard him as he spoke to David Dimbleby insert the work 'actually' between the word 'to' and the verb. I thought to myself: 'That man just split an infinitive, so he must be stupid.' To actually insert, or rather to insert actually, or more precisely, actually to insert the word 'actually' between the two parts of an infinitive, and I pause for you to be shocked again, is something up with which I shall not put. Whom did he think he was addressing? It was I.

The teaching of English is back in the news again, and the cosh has been brought out for both primary and secondary teachers. As you will know from reading the press, primary teachers do not give a fig for spelling, grammar or syntax, and secondary English teachers are all long-haired layabouts who think Tennyson is a brand of lager and Shelley is that blonde woman who sings with one of the pop bands. With teachers like that around, small wonder that Shakespeare could not even spell his own name correctly according to extant signatures. How he ever got around to composing all those funny cigar commercials after such an initial handicap, I shall never know.

David Pascall of the National Curriculum Council told teachers that they should be correcting children's speech errors in the playground. Now I don't know about you. Dave, but I tend to hesitate just a touch. However, I shall try. During my next football coaching session I shall make it clear that players must call out: 'To whom shall I pass?' When uncertain what to do with the ball. Should a brick come flying across the playground from the nearby building site, I shall urge them to shout: 'Harold, would you please beware of the heavy object speeding towards your cranium.' instead of the more common 'Duck, 'Arry'.

The only light relief in all this came in a document sent to schools recently headed *Rules for determining overall subject and profile component levels.* This is now being read in staffrooms around the land, and teachers are being wheeled off to the casualty department in droves, convulsed with mirth at the sheer elasticity of the English language. Savour the section on English assessment, telling how to derive the level for each Profile Component, then read it out loud to a friend.

'For PC1 (Speaking and listening): The PC level is the TA level. For PC2 (Reading): The PC level is the NC Test level. For PC3 (Writing): First examine the constituent **AT levels,** based on the **NC Test levels** and the **TA level** in the case of AT4/5: — If the TA in AT4/5 (Presentation) is at level 7 and the AT3 (writing) is at level 8, then the **PC level is the AT3 NC Test level:** if the TA in AT4/5 is not at level 7, but is **higher than level 4,** then the PC level is worked out as follows: AT3 NC test level x 8 **plus** AT4/5 TA level x 2. **Divide THIS TOTAL by 10** — if the NC Test level for ATs 4 and 5 is **at or below level 4.** the PC level is worked out as follows: AT3 Test level x 8 plus AT4 NC Test level **plus** AT5 Test level. **Divide THIS TOTAL by 10.'**

Some of us can remember when teaching was about helping children learn, and I swear I have not made up one word of this. Indeed, I would not have dared pen such consummate tripe for fear people would think I had gone right over the abyss. It is 100 per cent genuine national curriculum bullshit. Satire nowadays, especially where Government pronouncements on the teaching of English are concerned, is unnecessary. You just have to copy bits out of official documents.

I am sorry the right-wing has tried to seize the moral high ground on such matters as spelling, as I have always been keen on the matter myself. Indeed, I am the pedantic prig who goes round inserting the missing 'm' in notices where the writer has spelled 'accommodation' incorrectly. Poor old John Patten, however has to put it at the very top of his agenda.

When he addressed university vice-chancellors last week, what was a short throwaway remark in the actual speech, about excluding candidates who were poor spellers, was given massive prominence in the press release to ensure headline treatment and another week of relief from powerful right-wing critics.

I shall be watching his speech to the party conference with great interest, as there is a Richter Scale on these matters. Mentioning 'grammar' registers at six, though 'syntax' only scores three and 'use the gerund correctly' a mere one, as people are not sure what it is. 'Incompetent teachers' registers at eight and 'bring back corporal punishment' would get a nine. Wait for the moment when he says: 'We shall make all schools grant-maintained and cane teachers who do not correct spelling mistakes'. That will score a hundred and raise the roof of the hall.

Forget Peter Brough and Archie Andrews, Ray Alan and Lord Charles or any of the other great ventriloquists. To actually hammer English teaching, as Kenneth Clarke might say, to really suggest, as he might go on, that teachers are slack about grammar and spelling, to really and truly split your tights, let alone your infinitives, on this issue, will ensure a standing ovation and another few weeks of relief for the poor beggar from the hard right. Sit back and watch the best vent act on television. Study the platform party carefully. Not a lip will be seen moving. Somebody somewhere will be working him with his foot.

Times Educational Supplement 2.10.92

Erasmus performs to get his goat

I should like to become a schools inspector. Can any of your readers tell me how I set about it? I am 63 by the way.
I M Doolally, Coventry.

My grandfather has just become a schools inspector so I know exactly what happens. You have to write to Help the Aged and then you are interviewed. So long as you know nothing about education, have a few prejudices (grandpa is a firm believer in caning), you can earn a few bob in your spare time. In fact, grandpa's dead. So come on, Mr Doolally get out of that bath chair and start inspecting! It's a nice little top-up to the pension.
B Dross, Surbiton.

What is performance-related pay and where can you get it?
S O Hardup, Bath.

Performance-related pay goes back to classical times. Lucian describes how, in Greece, teachers were given three extra kippers if they filled in their dinner register properly. In Roman times Quintilian was paid a bottle of wine for every year 2 pupil who reached level 4 of the SATs in oratory. Erasmus was given a goat for understanding the national curriculum technology syllabus, and the natives of the Galapagos Islands paid Darwin 10 iguanas for externally moderating the key stage 3 Shakespeare paper. The governor of Monte Cristo gaol earned extra cash for coming top of the truancy league until the Count escaped.
Professor U Pedant, University of Life.

You get performance-related pay by performing, as I keep telling the chimps!
Billy Smart, The Big Top, second marquee on the right, a field in Hertfordshire.

I am told there is another Education Bill going through Parliament. Can someone explain to me exactly what is in it, as I haven't read it?
K Clarke, The Nag's Head.

Your reader must be referring to the 1993 The Minister Can Do Whatever He Wants (Education) Bill which is currently going through the House of Lords. The crucial clause is number 99 (c) (iii), which reads: 'In the aforementioned education system the Minister can, should he so deem, enact whatsoever he may please under whatever conditions and however demented, so sucks to you.' Basically it is part of the Government's policy to strengthen parental choice. Parents who vote against opting out can choose whether to be put up against a wall and shot, or be locked in a room for a month with all the national curriculum documents.
B Loopy-Drawers, Department for Education.

I have read about this Mum's Army of one-year trained infant school teachers, but I have just retired from a firm of snow shovellers, and I should like to know if dads are eligible as well.
I M Gormless, Wigan.

The Mum's Army idea is my own and I am proud of it. Anyone can join — mums, dads, window cleaners, prime ministers, snow shovellers — so long as you have no education and a few weeks to spare for a course which we haven't worked out yet (but don't worry, it's only teaching the little ones!), you will be welcome. I decided that since I only had a couple of O-levels myself (in knitting and bean growing), it was only fair that no one else should have the opportunity to be educated properly. After all, look where it has got me, the most popular prime minister ever. Oh yes!
J Major, Downing Street.

I am a primary school pupil and my school is opting out. What have I to look forward to?
L Red Riding-Hood.

Tea with grandma.
The Wolf.

Key stages 3 and 4.
Cynic (name and address supplied).

Why did those nasty heads boo the nice Secretary of State at the National Association of Head Teachers conference in Newcastle?
J Patten, Neverneverland.

I was present at the NAHT conference and I can honestly say that the press reports of the event were greatly exaggerated. Whereas the Daily Globe reported: 'When the heroic Mr Patten said how much he cared for young children, a thousand hippy-beaded Marxist heads screamed

'Get off the stage, you prat' as they viciously kicked the saintly minister with their open toed sandals,' the truth was that one grey-suited head muttered 'Oh, come now', when Mr Patten said, 'You will all eat dirt, you scumbags, and like it.' The press has a lot to answer for.
L Trotsky, Gulag Junior School, Harrogate.

How can I influence Government education policy?
A Busybody, Bexley.

Buy a dictionary and a pin. Become a minister.
Anon (signature indecipherable).

What is government education policy?
450,000 teachers, England and Wales.

Join us.
Col. Adam Smith-Rightwinger, Campaign to Stuff the Bastards.

Coming next week:

Am I remembered with affection?
Kenneth Baker, Greasy Pole

Who am I?
E Blatch, House of Lords.

What the hell is the Government doing to my plays?
Wm Shakespeare, Stratford.

Who shat on my SAT?
Confused, SEAC.

Times Educational Supplement 25.6.93

What a load of spherical objects?

One of my favourite BBC schools programmes is *Watch*, a blockbuster for young children taken by about 80 per cent of our primary schools. If you visit several schools and discover the head, the teachers, the caretaker, the pupils and half the parents dressed up as Roman soldiers chasing each other up and down the school playground, there is a sporting chance that *Watch* is doing the Romans.

The other week *Watch* had another great idea. The topic was 'Round and round', and according to the programme blurb teachers should encourage children to look out for round and spherical objects in their everyday life. Brilliant. My whole life consists entirely nowadays of round and spherical objects. Indeed, assigning a Cobblers Factor of one to ten to everything in the daily post or the newspapers is the only thing that keeps me going. Some mornings everything I read earns a CF from five up to ten.

A load of spherical objects arrived recently from the Higher Education Funding Council. I can warn anyone thinking of opting out that life with a Funding Council is not exactly a bundle of laughs. Government policy can be translated directly into action without appearing to have passed through a single brain on the way. Everything in universities nowadays is audited to death. The letter from the Funding Council asking us to apply for 'quality ratings' in teaching made it the *sixth* different audit of teaching and research that we would undergo in this academic year. Even fans of accountability find it utterly ridiculous.

I keep wondering how the great creative figures of history would have reacted to constant audit. Imagine the phone calls: 'Hello, is that Ludwig van Beethoven? Look, Ludwig, do you mind if I just pop round and audit your *Moonlight Appassionata*? What's that? I don't care if some French bloke has just been in to audit another of your sonatas and called it *pathétique*. Alright then, there's no need to be rude. I will pop round and 'pester bloody Schubert' as you put it. And it's no use pretending you're deaf, by the way'. Or alternatively: 'That was quite a good speech, Mr Churchill, and I liked the bit about fighting them on the beaches, but you don't seem to have listed your outcome objectives in your lesson notes'.

There have been some interesting examples of spherical objects from a former Secretary of State for Education in the topicial field of reading. You will recall that Kenneth Clarke, bless him, was always quick to condemn teachers on the teaching of reading, and we always assumed that Clarkie was dead serious about the subject and must be a keen reader himself. I was a bit sorry for the poor chap, therefore — no, I tell a lie I herniated myself laughing — when it was revealed that he had not actually read the Maastricht Treaty. It reminded me of the farewell poem I penned to him in *The TES* when he left the DFE:

> 'Everything on one sheet of A4'
> Was your motto.
> Why didn't you read them?

My advice to anyone running out of local management of schools money is to write on a piece of paper 'I hereby give the bearer of this document one trillion pounds of government money', and then simply go up to the great man and ask him to sign it. With his impeccable record for careful reading your problems are over.

A lorry load of round objects some with a CF right at the very top of the range, has come from John Patten recently. His lips can move in strange and mysterious ways, depending on who is actually working the Muppet that day, but he has come out with some belters. Remember his justification for taking out over a million school places and closing down several schools along the way? It would allow more money for teachers' pay, we were told — like 1½ per cent. A CF of ten for that one.

Then there was the statement that grant-maintained schools would get a quarter of the capital building programme in education though they currently constitute just 1½ per cent of the schools one and a half marks out of a hundred and a CF of nine seems a fair score for that kind of equity. Another 'idea' straight from his market-mad right-wing manipulators came out when he told a journalist that if trainee teachers were pushed straight into classrooms without training, schools could buy in any necessary higher education. No higher education institution would simply sit around on the off-chance that a school might ring up one day, so it would either close down, or more likely go and do something else instead, thereby detaching teaching from higher education at the very moment when the rest of Europe is moving in the opposite direction.

But the biggest CF must be awarded to the House of Commons over the 1992 Education Bill. I wonder when some MPs will realise that the 'Yah, boo, sucks to you' style of debate might not even have been all that wonderful in the lower-sixth debating club, let alone the country's major decision-making chamber. A typical exchange reads as follows in *Hansard*:

> **Mr Patten:** Why will the hon. Gentleman not let the Under-secretary respond? He is frightened.

> **Madam Deputy Speaker:** Order. The class is getting restless.

Top drawer debate, eh? After numerous such spherical objects they troop through the lobbies like cattle to vote, irrespective of the points made. A load of bullocks if you ask me.

Times Educational Supplement 27.11.92

I am not a free man,
I am a number

Two questions: do you remember that popular but mysterious televi-
sion series, now being repeated on Channel 4, called *The Prisoner*?
Second, do you remember Egon Krenz, or for that matter Manfred
Gerlach, or Gregor Gysi? I shall return to the second question later, but
I watched an episode of *The Prisoner* the other week, and for the first
time I began to understand what it was all about.

When *The Prisoner* was first shown in the 1960s it soon became a cult.
Pages of print were produced speculating about its meaning, as week
after week poor old Patrick McGoohan, known simply as 'Number 6',
tried to escape from 'the Village', a closed community where strange
characters wandered around and a disembodied loudspeaker voice
barked out invocations to be happy and enjoy yourself.

All the viewer knew was that the Prisoner, or Number 6, resigned
from some government department, was sent to the Village, was trying
to escape, and that every week when he nearly succeeded, he either
found it was all a dream, or a huge white bubble came and flattened
him.

It was only when I saw an episode about how inhabitants of the
Village are compelled to watch a television programme which will bring
them up to degree level in history in just three minutes of intensive
brainwashing, that I realised the awful truth. The interpretation became
crystal clear and all speculation can now end. The giveaway was the bit
about getting a degree in three minutes. The whole show had to be about
Government education policy. It wants universities to cut down degree
courses from three years to two, but three minutes would do nicely.

The rest then falls neatly into place. The Prisoner is, of course, John
Patten. The mysterious government department in which he used to
work is the Home Office, where he was the only junior minister to stay
for five years without anyone even inviting him into the Cabinet Room
for a cup of tea. The Village is the expensive new headquarters of the

Department for Education, the inappropriately named Sanctuary Buildings, with its ridiculous palm trees and tinkling fountain.

The Prisoner, John Patten, is held in captivity by right-wing nasties. Why is he called Number 6? Simple. He followed the Famous Five — Mark (Who?) Carlisle, Lord Come-back-all-is-forgiven Joseph, Greasy Baker, John MacGregor and the odious Clarke. The large white bubble? Equally obvious. It has been sent by the Right to flatten him if he dares to reject their loony ideas or to step out of line. The reason he is shown sprinting across the beach faster than Linford Christie at the beginning of each episode? He is terrified it will roll over him and ruin his bouffant hair-do.

If more proof were needed, take his daft 1992 Education Bill. It is 200 pages of the most monumental bureaucratic bullshit, but all the right-wing ideas are in it. There are 138 clauses, more than half the Bill, about grant-maintained schools — when governors can clip their toe-nails, what will happen if they go bust, what they should do if the ballcock in the head's private toilet seizes up — all this for just over 1 per cent of the total number of schools.

For the other 99 per cent, there are a few clauses on what the hit squad will do to you if you are thought to be failing. If you are really bad you will be forced to become a grant-maintained school. I can just see the letter from Bouffant Boy: 'Dear Head, Your school is so bad I have decided to compel you to opt out. If parents point out that the word 'opt' normally means 'choose freely', tell them to bog off. Signed, Number 6, the Prisoner.

Then there are the clauses giving him the power to compel local authorities to close schools, concealed under less aggressive language such as 'rationalisation', 'discontinuance of schools' and 'remedying the excess of places'. There is no sanctuary for grant-maintained schools (yes, it's them again, folks), as he can shut those down directly through the 'Funding Agency' that will administer them, which will in any case be the Minister's poodle, and will probably be chaired by Colonel Adam Smith-Rightwinger or Lady Rotating-Eyeballs.

A few years ago, education ministers joked that they only had the power to close temporary buildings in school playgrounds. Kenneth Baker soon changed that by taking over 400 powers, and the Blow-dry Kid is stacking up a few more, making at least 500 in all. Number 6 can now tell you exactly how many beads must be counted out into how many piles when giving Standard Assessment Tasks to seven-year-olds; precisely when and, no doubt, before long how — you must teach the building technology of the Parthenon, or medieval poets' use of bee symbolism; and he can shut you down if he doesn't like the look of you. This enormous power would be bad enough if he had a single idea of his own, but when he is merely the well coiffured front man for invisible right-wing manipulators, it is terrifying.

And Egon Krenz? He was the poor beggar who was head of East Germany for just a few months in 1989, during which time he was seen on television looking totally bewildered. He resigned at the end of the year and was succeeded by Manfred Gerlach and Gregor Gysi. All three have now passed into the Encyclopaedia of Nonentities, where they will one day be joined in complete oblivion by the man who will receive his due reward for bowing the knee uncritically to the right-wing — the Egon Krenz of British educational history, the Prisoner, Number 6 — John Who-the-hell-was-he?

Times Educational Supplement 13.11.92

Ted's guide to festive frolics

As Christmas draws nearer and the excitement grows, here are a few happy tips to help you prepare for the festive season.

Ideas for Presents

For him

Bouffant Boy Wig Kit: Weave-it-yourself authentic John Patten wig with double bouffant blow wave. Genuine horse hair, looks like the real thing. The man in your life will look a right wally wearing it. Hours of harmless pleasure £8.99, *all DIY shops*

For Her

National Curriculum Quilt: Knit your very own national curriculum. Ten separate pieces to be knitted or crocheted, but since some are round, some square, some star-shaped, they don't actually fit together! Watch her grow more and more frustrated trying to turn it into a quilt. One big laugh for spectators. £9.99. *NCC Enterprises*

For the kids

Horror Ken-Masks: Realistic looking face masks of Kenneth Baker and Kenneth Clarke. Kids everywhere love putting them on and then leaping out unexpectedly in front of their teacher shouting, 'Cooee, I'm back!'. Free resuscitation pack and heart defibrillator with every mask. £5.99, *or £7.99 for de luxe version (with real slime), Ken-Masks, Ministerial Clones Corp.*

Festive games

Redundo: Jolly snakes-and-ladders-type game for teachers. Win and lose points for being young and cheap, or experienced and expensive. Try to outsmart your opponents and get them fired. When someone reaches the top square, everyone leaps up and shouts 'Redundo!' Last player left wins game and becomes chairman of governors. Hilarious fun. £14.99 *(free dole cheques included in box),* some LEAs.

Cock Up: Make-up exam scores for a set of schools and league-table them. A real side-splitter. Players fake scores and even invent schools that don't exist. If anyone complains about your errors you simply blame the schools. ('Loved it'. *John Patten;* 'Most agreeable, I think, but I'm not sure', *John Major*). £1.99, DFE Games Inc.

Just Testing: Write questions on abstruse aspects of algebra and physics and then make seven-year-olds answer them. Watch them struggle with Quantum Theory and Boolean algebra. ('Laugh? I tiddled myself', *various ministers*). £2.99, SEAC.

Complete Bullocks: Invent your own stupid idea, write it up in ridiculous bureaucratic language, pass an Education Act making it law, and then send it to the nearest school with 20 forms to return. Sit back and watch the head and all the teachers have a nervous breakdown trying to fill in the forms *and teach at the same time!* Hysterical fun. £19.99, *Marquis de Sade Games Plc.*

Entertainment

Pantomine
Prat in Boots starring John Patten as Dick Head, the ambitious down-and-going politician, and Nora Batty as Baroness Blatch. *Theatre of the Absurd, Sanctuary Buildings, at least twice daily.*

Films on TV
Carry On Committee (Boxing Day. BBC1). *The Carry On* team favourites become members of national committees for education and complete mayhem ensures. All the usual *double entendres* ('How about us completing a few attainment targets then, ducky?' 'I wouldn't like to bump into *his* profile component") as Colonel Adam Smith-Rightwinger (Kenneth Williams) chairs a committee responsible for reforming curriculum and testing. Brilliant cameo appearance as amateur school inspector Mr Porkchop (Kenneth Clarke).

Opt Out (New Year's Eve, Channel 4). Hollywood disaster movie about a school that opts out and then falls down a disused mine shaft. Clint Eastwood stars as Tough Toenails, the minister who doesn't give a monkey's, with Oscar winning song *'What kind of fool was I?'* sung by chairman of governors (Anthony Newley).

Food tips

What do you suggest as a cure for post-Xmas blues?
A SAT pack on the Rocks (two measures each of whisky, gin, vodka, brandy, tequila, lightly stirred with a slice of lemon, a cherry and lots of ice). It doesn't cure the blues, but it makes you believe you've already marked your SATs.

Do the 1992 Education Bill and a Xmas Turkey have anything in common?
Yes, two things: (1) the 1992 Education Bill is a turkey, (2) both need stuffing.

What's the best thing to do with vegetables?
Make them ministers.

Times Educational Supplement 11.12.92

Beware Horace, sound-bite trendy

One of the ploys the politicians have used against the teaching profession during the past few years has been to accuse them of being wild lunatics, espousing way-out ideologies and employing crackpot teaching methods. The notion is utterly laughable to anyone who has been into a single school, but in the politicians' *How to Slag Off Teachers* manual, it is firmly ensconced as tactic Number One.

In other countries teachers are seen as unrevolutionary people, keepers of the runes, respectable, middle-aged, earnestly getting on with their job, not exactly tearing down society. In Britain there is much sport to be had portraying these same professional people as gung-ho tearaways, pedagogical ramraiders, joyriding through the schoolyard in their souped-up 1974 Hillman Imps, ungratefully squandering their half per cent salary increase on silly Marxist tracts. The only convincing proof that teachers are hell bent on producing a nation of cretins is the behaviour of those who put the argument forward.

The truth of the matter is far removed from the image politicians seek to portray. Most teachers are over 40 and use a mixture of methods. Her Majesty's Inspectorate report on teaching reading concluded that three per cent of teachers used only phonics, and five per cent exclusively the so-called 'real books' approach. 'Most teachers and most pupils in most schools work hard,' was the opening statement of a press release on another HMI report.

Unfortunately many people do not have the chance to read such reports. Repeat the big lie often enough and it seeps into public consciousness. Individual teachers do not have the time, resources or access to the mass media to refute the untruths. The prevailing view among parents is: 'Our children's school is fine, but from what I hear it must be hell elsewhere.'

The public has been told by politicians that teachers are undermining the national curriculum (that's funny, I thought they were the ones teaching it), that protests about tests for 14- year-olds are being masterminded by a group of dangerous revolutionaries (presumably this includes those well-known urban guerrillas, the heads of independent schools), and that teacher-trainers are wild trendies (most of the ones I know are more like Doris Day than Che Guevara).

I have been trying to track down the origins of this misplaced revolutionary image. It is commonly believed to have started in many right-wing think-tank pamphlets attacking teachers and schools, which are avidly believed by the more gullible politicians. However, I have discovered the true story: prepare to be shocked.

The whole thing is down to one man. He is not generally known to the public, but his name is Horace Pumpernickel. His sole purpose in life is to follow ministers around calling out remarks for them to quote at press conferences as examples of wild trendiness. The other week there he was again winding up Lady Blatch, telling her that you couldn't teach *Romeo and Juliet* without teaching children about condoms.

It reminds me of scenes in the *Goon Show*, when Spike Milligan played Minnie Bannister, who went around crying: 'We'll all be murdered in our beds.' The conversation probably goes like this. Horace Pumpernickel: 'You can't teach *Romeo and Juliet* without mentioning condoms'; Lady Blatch: 'Help, help, a Marxist! We'll all be murdered in our beds'. Horace collapses with mirth at another successful jape. He was particularly active a few weeks ago. According to a newspaper report, Lady Blatch announced that a design and technology teacher (Horace again sporting a goatee beard) had said children were victims of the free market, and 'others described reading as 'a means of social control'.' (Horace, wearing platform heels and a safety pin through his nose: 'Ey up, missus. Reading is a means of social control'; Lady Blatch: 'Help, help, a Marxist. We'll all be murdered in our beds').

What is sinister about the latest co-ordinated attack is that it is softening up the public for John Patten's forthcoming announcement about teacher training. This may reveal, among other things, the John Major plan for students to be bunged into schools without any proper training and for mothers to train as primary teachers in one year on the job. When I was at school a lad called Brian was notorious because his mother always came into the playground to sort out anyone who had offended her lad. A year's training might at least have helped her pick out the right child to smack round the ear.

Mr Patten believes that 'left-wing ideology, still strong in schools and teacher training colleges, has contributed to a decline in standards', according to one newspaper report. He is said to be 'alarmed that it is becoming increasingly difficult to find well-trained young staff'. Hold on a minute. Did not a recent report say the reason schools were appointing so many teachers straight from training was not just cheapness, but because they are well trained? However, let us not spoil prejudice with facts.

Compare the education watch-dog Ofsted's press release on the articled and licensed teacher schemes with the Department for Education version. The HMI said the licensed teacher scheme was not well structured, did not always match trainees' needs, was supported less than satisfactorily, and was only rescued because of teachers' goodwill. The articled teachers' scheme, which lasted twice as long and cost three times as much as normal training, was 'not significantly different from the standards found in conventional PGCE courses'. Lady Blatch hailed the report as a 'major boost for the Government's plans'. HMI is astonished at this 'interesting' interpretation.

I am setting up a task force to deal with Horace Pumpernickel called British Ladies Against Teachers Called Horace. We at Blatch will continue to hammer the profession. It's the language they understand. If you haven't been Blatched, you're nobody.

Times Educational Supplement 5.3.93

Wimps who think they are Tarzan

Recent education ministers have been like Russian dolls — inside each was a smaller one waiting to emerge. When they eventually split their chrysalis, out comes not a beautiful butterfly, but an even smaller twerp. Apart from John MacGregor, who broke the chain of ever diminishing gumption by showing the ability to listen, think and then manage and who will therefore go down in the fossil record as a mutant, each of the last three ministers hs been worse than his predecessor. It is the kind of evolution that Darwin called 'survival of the twittest'.

If you want to see the origins of all the turmoil currently afflicting schools, look no further than the Baker-Clarke-Patten triumvirate. None could run the proverbial chip shop. Baker would at least have saved on the oil bills, Clarke would have told all his patrons they must eat beans on toast and like it, and Patten would have been so busy admiring himself in the mirror above the chip pan, he would not have noticed it was on fire. Then he would have told the press that he had had a warm welcome from his customers.

Each became a worse exponent of the outdated macho 'Me Tarzan, you dirt' style of management. Forget all the publicity hype from Baker about how he put Mrs Thatcher right. The truth is that he wanted every single attainment target in every single subject to be tested, so that parents of seven-year-olds would have received a head-spinning string of meaningless digits, instead of an informative profile of their children's progress.

When he was warned about the folly of this mad approach, he stood up at his party conference assuring the audience that he would plough on to the end of the furrow, no matter what anyone said. So he did, and with everyone yelling 'Switch off the plough, you idiot', proceeded to carve a huge divot straight through the flower bed, up the stairs and right through the middle of the Persian carpet .

John MacGregor tried to repair the damage and see how the national curriculum could be implemented sensibly, but the next Russian doll, Kenneth Clarke decided he was an expert on the English language and told the world that he had buried the Plowden Report. Since he had clearly read it as carefully as it later turned out he had read the Maastricht Treaty, this caused great hilarity. But his aimless blundering through ill-understood territory simply compounded the problem and stored up more trouble for later, as did his awful manner towards professional people.

I warned a senior police officer I know that, with his penchant for telling doctors they were reaching for their wallet, and teachers that they were useless, it would only be a matter of time before Clarkie said that he wanted a reform of the police service and would root out incompetent police officers. Sure enough he had done both by Christmas and the police are currently in exactly the same state of turmoil and loss of confidence that doctors and teachers were in. Any sizeable profession will have its share of less competent practitioners, but only a meathead starts off his management strategy by implying that all are members of this minority. It is a nakedly crude control tactic.

Just when it seemed there could be no smaller doll, even within the skin of the copious Clarke, out came Patten. Unfortunately, international footballer Paul Gascoigne has already appropriated the best book title for describing this three-man dynasty, as his biography is entitled *Daft as a Brush*, but to have a trio of superstars like Bazza, Clazza, and now Pazza, is really too much for the education system to bear.

Pazza began by disappearing. Indeed there were rumours that he did not exist at all, but was just a hologram. Then, after his disastrous slagging off of representatives of parents' groups as having Neanderthal views, someone obviously took him on one side an told him to get a haircut and go on radio and television and talk properly to people. Since then he has never been off it — morning, lunchtime, evening radio, television, even *Blue Peter* ('Today we we hoping to have the education minister, but here's one I made earlier')

Look out for cameo appearances as Captain Troy in *Thunderbirds are Go!* Gary on *Blind Date* and the lead role in *Tarzan beats up the Association of Teachers and Lecturers*. Managing to goad the gentle and highly responsible members of the ATL into unanimously supporting a ballot on test boycotts, by suggesting they were wimps who had given him an easy ride, was a rare piece of perverse genius, the equivalent of getting St Francis of Assisi to kick his pet dog.

The sad thing is that being a good minister is not all that hard. It requires key stage 1 language competence, involving a vocabulary no more difficult than 'I'm listening', 'That's a good point', 'What do you think about . . .', 'Please' and 'Thank you'. There is no point in uttering empty words that on the surface appear to pay tribute to teachers if they are inevitably followed by a 'But . . .' that suggests the profession is malevolent, unpatriotic, irresponsible or incompetent.

The next step is to have a bit of imagination and ability to solve problems, but again it is only at key stage 1, as the world is full of people who have good and workable ideas. Pazza should capitalise on these. Only Lord Keith comeback-all-is-forgiven Joseph appears to have had the ability to say that someone else had a good idea. Perhaps we should found a 'Proud to be a Wimp' movement as an antidote to all this blind machismo.

My final piece of advice to Pazza is also very simple key stage 1 stuff. Stop looking so bloody smug all the time.

Times Educational Supplement 30.4.93

Petrified by prehistoric methods

I can't wait to see Steven Spielberg's next blockbuster movie, *Jurassic Park* 2. Capitalising on the successful theme of restoring the past, it tells of a scientist who finds a mosquito which has been enclosed in a piece of amber since 1854, discovers it contains the blood of Mr M'Choakum-child from *Hard Times* by Charles Dickens, extracts the DNA, manufactures several clones of the Victorian schoolmaster, puts them all in the Government and on national committees responsible for education, and recreates the glories of the Victorian age in 1993.

There are spectacular scenes where the clones rampage through the education system brutally killing off local authorities, re-establishing payment by results, insisting that children chant slogans all day long about, in the words of Dickens in *Hard Times*, ' the watersheds of all the world (whatever they are) and all the histories of all the peoples and all the names of all the rivers and the mountains, and all the productions, manners and customs of all the countries, and all their boundaries and bearings on the two and thirty points of the compass'. Most of us know it better as key stages 2 and 3. There seems to have been a great fear in Victorian times that children might possibly think for themselves and that this would be deeply threatening to the very foundations of society. In order to prevent this horror, individualism was frowned upon and children were encouraged to chant in unison. In the history books there are photographs of a class of children, all of whom have drawn an identical picture of a fly, copied on to their slates from the blackboard. I know that nowadays one child would draw a picture and fax it to the rest, but I like to think there is a bit of encouragement to children to express their individuality in the late 20th century.

Dissent and nonconformity were strongly discouraged in Victorian schools, as they are by some people today. Teachers are pressurised not to express reservations or protest about what they are asked to do, even if it goes against their professional judgement. It is noteworthy that the teachers who have aroused greatest wrath from the Victorian throw-backs are those who teach English, so a foundation stone of their education has been critical analysis and the penetration of deception and dissimulation.

It is interesting to look at some of the tasks children are asked to do in school to see what kind of thinking they need to engage in. In one book there was a picture of a painting by Van Gogh of the interior of his house. Underneath were several questions children had to answer about this great I work of art. The one that creased me up was: Did Van Gogh wear a hat?' It sounded like the title of a surreal novel. More to the point, I suppose, would have been: 'And when he chopped his ear off, did it slip down over one eye?

Why stop there? The Government sees unchallenge as the order of the day, hence its emphasis on narrow factual learning, anxiety about children tackling controversial issues, great fear of teachers thinking for themselves and being anything other than faithful implementers of the national curriculum and the Government's tests. So how about other possibilities? Did Rembrandt wear braces? Did Michelangelo prefer Dulux? Did Einstein use a Biro? Was Beethoven's ear trumpet made of brass? Did Sir Francis Drake wear Y-fronts? Did Shakespeare like ham sandwiches? There is no limit to banality.

Perhaps the explanation of the Government's preference for passive teaching and learning lies partly in the observation of a foreign visitor who came to see me after he had visited a number of British cities.

He was very impressed at the dedication of the teachers he had seen working in such difficult conditions, and astonished that there should be so much rubbishing of inner-city teachers from politicians, but he was also deeply shocked at what he had observed — decrepit housing, high unemployment, ancient crumbling schools. 'What I can't understand,' he said, 'is why people don't riot every day.' All this tinder box needs is a demagogue who says, 'Don't stand for it friends — to the barricades!', and the whole thing would go up and blow Van Gogh's hat off.

Let us hope *Jurassic Park 3* will be about the scientist who finds a mosquito enclosed in a piece of amber and discovers it contains the blood of another kind of Victorian, Joseph Chamberlain, so he creates a batch of clones who then knock down all the old houses and schools and build brand new ones, fit for people to live and be educated in.

As the summer term draws to a close, keep an eye out for the usual launch of controversial proposals just as the last teacher is leaving for a weekend break in Stoke, or what ever people are squandering their princely pay rise on this year. Will the Dearing Committee cut down the straitjacketing verbiage of the national curriculum? Will my prediction that the original 17 attainment targets in science, (which dropped to five, then four) would one day be reduced to three (chemistry, physics and biology), even one (science), come true? Will teachers be encouraged to think for themselves, and their pupils likewise? And will Van Gogh at last find his wretched hat?

In the meantime, enjoy the boarding house in Stoke. Try to resist giving a national curriculum level to the breakfast sausage, proposing performance-related pay for the waiters, voting to boycott the afternoon tea, and worrying about the great questions in contemporary teaching and learning, such as whether Van Gogh liked cornflakes. Instead let us declare a short interlude before it all starts again in September, pausing only to wish education ministers well and offer them just one piece of advice: Stay away from mosquitoes. I hate to think what *Jurassic Park 4* would be like.

Times Educational Supplement 23.7.93

Chapter 2

Mad Curriculum Disease

Follies that confound the SATirists

I knew in the summer that satire was in for a hard time. The local newspaper headline 'NATs to replace SATs', telling the world about the 'new assessment tasks' for seven-year-olds, tolled the bell for staffroom satirists everywhere. I mean, what on earth is the point of busting a gut to invent BATs (Bizarre Assessment Tasks) and PRATs (Particularly Relevant Assessment Tasks), when the government machine is working overtime to devise NATs? This has to constitute unfair competition.

Furthermore, why bother making up the kind of bureaucratic legalese that gets crap a bad name when the Department of Education and Science will trump your ace every time? The document telling the world about testing seven-year-olds is called *The Education (National Curriculum) (Assessment Arrangements for English, Maths and Science) (Key Stage 1) Order 1991*. This is a three bracket job, way above the head of your average satirist.

Or take the deathless gems of the text itself: 'If, in the circumstances to which paragraph (2)(c) applies, the application of the level of attainment determined by the teacher assessment in accordance with article 7 would produce a different profile component level from that which such an application of the level determined by the SAT assessment would produce, the level of attainment determined by the teacher assessment shall, if the local authority (in the case of a school which the authority maintains) or SEAC (in the case of a grant-maintained school) determine that it represents the more accurate assessment of the pupil's achievements, be the level for the purposes of article 7.' Now have you got that, for goodness' sake? I shan't tell you again. No wonder the Satirists' Union has called a one-day strike in protest.

It is quite astonishing how the testing of seven-year-old children has moved from being a gleam in the eye of the market-mad right wing a few years ago, to a central political issue today. At each stage along the way national testing has been used as yet another excuse for teacher bashing. First, during the debates of the 1988 Education Bill, it was said by one minister that teachers' opposition to national tests was through fear of quality control. There were dark hints that SATs would expose teachers as the generous softies they were, festooning high grades on their pupils for any old rubbish. The SATs would reveal how incompetent children really were. Originally, then, the prediction was that SATs would come out *lower* than teacher assessments.

The first analyses of the pilots suggested that SAT scores were, if anything, *higher* than teacher assessments. Was this followed by a fulsome apology, an assertion that teachers were rigorous in their assessments, that the SATs may be too simple? No, ministers sought to set parents against teachers by suggesting that the latter did not recognise their children's talent, only the SATs could. It is a touching faith in the power of a single test, as if only teachers' judgement is frail.

More rubbishing took place when the Government decreed that refusal to co-operate with the new privatised inspectors be a criminal offence with a fine of £1,000, suggesting that teachers were crooks. If you really want to blow a grand, nip down to Ladbroke's is my advice.

Then there was the outcry when the first analysis of SAT scores gave the distributions over levels 1, 2 and 3. 'A quarter of children below average' was one headline. Personally, I shall not rest until 100 per cent of children are above average, or at least until 100 per cent of the population understands what 'average' actually means. Funny, I thought that having roughly a quarter below average, about a half average and a quarter above average, was what was known as a 'normal distribution', whether of test scores, height, or the consumption of chips.

That did not stop Clarkie rushing in to suggest that 28 per cent of children could not read. It was fair enough to point out that the levels were not actually based on a normal distribution, but rather on specific achievement criteria. However, if he had taken the trouble to look at his own national curriculum in English (too much to expect perhaps) he would have seen that level 1 does not mean complete inability to read. He might also have indicated that in many European countries children of six-and-a-half have only just started school, but we mustn't expect miracles from a level 1 minister.

So what are seven-year-olds in for this year? Well, let me clarify the new arrangements. First, the tests will be *simpler*. There will be four levels instead of three, technology will be added to the three core subjects as a further option and they will be spread over twice as many weeks. Teachers with any sense will ask for their salary and pension to be made *simpler* along similar lines.

There has been a great deal of misunderstanding about other features. For example, it is said that John Major has insisted on more 'pencil-and-paper' tests. Children will be given a pencil and asked to wrap it in a piece of paper. This is part of Government policy for early years' vocational education. There has also been much confusion over the Government's attitude to GCSE coursework. It was all based on a misprint, as the relevant paper should have read 'coarse work'. Seven-year-olds can earn between 20 and 30 per cent of their marks for being really uncouth, though Kenneth Clarke is firmly against 100 per cent being awarded for tasteless vulgarity to anyone other than himself.

Finally, they will be asked to implement the Citizen's Charter and remove motorway cones, inspect schools, that sort of thing. Oh, and by the way the 'floating and sinking' test has not been scrapped, as reported in the press, it has merely been modified. Seven-year-olds will be required to place their teachers in a sea of national curriculum documents to see if they float or sink and then make a league table of the results. Don't laugh. Just remember that the real BATs and PRATs are stranger than satire nowadays.

Times Educational Supplement 29.11.91

Don't shoot, I'm only the SAT tracker

There is that moment in all the best cowboy films, you will know it well, when the hero, a clean-cut matinée idol wearing smartly creased trousers and an absolutely spotless cream shirt, (even though he is supposed to have spent the last week riding furiously through Death Valley), straps on his gun belt and mutters some variant on. 'A man's gotta do what a man's gotta do'.

Then, pausing only to thump the living daylights out of the poor beggar acting as look-out man for Big Jake, a walk-on part now regularly performed by fired HMIs or senior civil servants who have crossed Kenneth Clarke, he strides purposefully towards the showdown.

I felt a little bit like that the other week when I received my key stage 1 SAT pack from the School Examinations and Assessment Council. For those who have not yet had the dubious pleasure of receiving a national testing kit at the start of the hunting season, let me explain what it involves.

One day your local postman, by now on his third free NHS truss, arrives at school like Santa bearing yet another huge sack of glossy brochures from SEAC. The first of these has on the front a colour photo of children sitting round a table clearly having tremendous fun drawing pictures. I cannot imagine how this happy, dare I say 'progressive' photo, gets past government censors, or why they are not sitting in rows doing a spelling test, but I digress.

The tone of the contents is inevitably jaunty. The principal message is that you are a member of a big happy club, like the sort that kids join where you send in your postal order and get your Little Twinky badge, useful plastic thingummy and membership card. But as fully paid up members of the SEAC Fun Fun Fun Club you get grown-up thingamajigs, such as your SAT pack, your source (or should it be 'sauce'?) sheets and your SAT trackers. Honest, I am not making this up, ask any infant school teacher. Cowboys strap on their gunbelts and track down unsuspecting villains, teachers strap on their SAT packs and track down unsuspecting seven-year-olds.

'What on earth is a SAT tracker?' I hear you ask. Well, it is one of nine jolly sets of baubles you get in your SAT pack. It is a double pull-out sheet covered in '*level*' this and '*part*' that. It has more arrows than were loosed at the Battle of Little Bit Horn, and looks for all the world like a game of Snakes and Ladders, except that it is all snakes and no ladders. The instructions on the cover say: 'The SAT trackers have been designed to help you to 'keep track' of your pupils as you regroup them'. Thanks SEAC, you're a pal. I'm always losing pupils when I re-group them. Some fall down the widening cracks in the floorboards, others just mutter, 'You're not regrouping me, mate, so shove your SAT pack', and go home.

Unlike Chief Sitting Bull, however, SAT trackers have three kinds of arrow, the YES+ arrow, the YES arrow and the NO arrow. According to the instructions you must use the NO arrow 'when a pupil does not complete the Part of the Activity, having stopped at an exit point'. So there you have it. Some hapless seven-year-old stops to tie his bootlace next to the fire escape, and bang, the poor beggar spends the rest of his life with a NO arrow stuck in his bum, being hunted down by the SAT trackers so he can be re-grouped. It's what we pay our taxes for, I suppose.

The tone of all this is firmly established in the cover sheet listing the contents of Santa's bumper parcel. 'This pack is all that teachers need to prepare themselves for conducting the 1992 standard assessment task'. Come again, SEAC. Did you say *all* that teachers need? Hold on a sec. It does go on to say, 'If any items are missing...contact the local authority assessment coordinator'.

Well, SEAC, I will be dropping a note to the said person. I seem not to have received such vital little items as the 500 pill pack of Librium, the two litre bottle of VAT 69, the box of amphetamines, and my free copies of the two government pamphlets on (1) *Which Prat Thought All This Up?* and (2) *Sex For The Debilitated* (HMSO 1992).

I was a little intrigued by the other statement on the cover sheet, 'Further packs for any purpose other than the statutory assessment are available'. What could this mean? Are they available ready-perforated for anyone who has run out of kitchen roll? Are there people who read them for enjoyment, in which case should they not just be referred to their GP or nearest Sanctuary for the Seriously Confused?

Incidentally, SEAC, before I forget, thanks also for the booklet on how to assess English. Now let me make sure I have got this right. I start by playing them a tape of the story *Hairy Bear* where Mrs Hairy Bear says 'Hairy Bear, Hairy Bear, I can hear robbers' and Hairy Bear replies, 'I don't care, I don't care. I'll fim-fam-fight 'em'.

Yes, I'm OK, I think, so far. But tell me, how did you get this past Kenneth Clarke? After all 'fim-fam-fight 'em' is not exactly Queen's English. Ah, I see. It's all an allegory of when Mrs Thatcher put Clarke in charge of education.

Well, SEAC, I think I've got it all under control now. I'll set off with my SAT tracker and fim-fam-fight 'em for you until they agree to be re-grouped. I can't wait to see all the stuff you'll be sending me for SATs at key stages 3 and 4. Assessing secondary pupils in 10 subjects at 10 levels in this neat manner should be fun, fun, fun, so will you make sure there are plenty of spare SAT trackers and a few dozen extra arrows in my SAT pack?

'Easy peasy. There's absolutely nothing to worry about', as General Custer once remarked.

Times Educational Supplement 21.2.92

THAT'S MY SAT TRACKER

Hide under the table and plead sanity

It has been a testing time for schools recently. The dominance of the 'test it if it moves' ethic in education nowadays is confirmed by the typical teacher's day. Everything is assessed, even when mentally still in pyjamas, so the day starts with a level 5 breakfast, followed by a level 1 journey to work, a level 3 roll call, a level 4 assembly, a few lessons ranging from level 1 to level 10, a level 2 staff meeting, a level 1 journey home, and a few hours of preparation and marking worth anything from level 10 down to level W.

In fact, level W is an interesting concept. It is the level given to someone not yet at level 1, the sort of grade you would give to the School Examinations and Assessment Council itself. It reminds me of the report written by a former colleague on a hapless pupil's performance in his English classes, which read: 'He is almost ready to start to think.' Applied to pupils the W means 'working towards level 1', in the case of SEAC it stands for something else which eludes me at the moment.

I was interested in the whole notion of W-ness when I opened eagerly, as I always do, my thick wad of papers from SEAC. Oh, the effable excitement of receiving one of these mailings. My joy was, as ever, uncontained at the prospect of yet more unpredictable mirth at the oodles of giggles, the acres of chuckles these pages would reveal. Why, when the BBC is crying out for decent comedy shows, these packages are not just shoved as they stand straight on to prime-time TV and radio with not a word altered is beyond me. Surely in these competitive times either BBC or ITV can find space on the airwaves for '*Allo 'Allo SEAC*, or *Only Fools and Teachers*, or even *One SAT in the Grave*.

Anyway, this latest rib-tickler, entitled *School assessment folder 1993 — key stage 1*, did not disappoint. No one is fooled by the neat typographical layout. Yes, there are indeed lots of blue bullets in the margin to highlight key points, blue code numbers, and blue type in blue shaded boxes. I suppose the subliminal approach is a lot subtler than actually writing 'Vote Conservative' in huge capitals at the top of each page, but I digress. Despite these nifty graphical devices, the text is as drivel-laden as ever.

Take the following, in the tradition of modern satire simply transcribed from page B3.3, a bureaucratic belter: 'Where there are three or more statements of attainment at a level, however, only those children who are successful on all of them are required to attempt the next level. There will be some cases therefore where teachers award a level on, say, two out of three successes, and the child is not required to attempt the next level. Conversely, where a child fails to attain a level, he or she must be assessed at the next lower level, if one is available. There is of course no limit to the number of levels you can offer children; higher and lower levels can be assessed whenever you think it would be beneficial.'

What the bloody hell does all this crap mean? What worries me, as I, along with thousands of others, am rushed by ambulance to the newly re-opened Mad Curriculum Disease isolation wards, is that there must be people out there who actually understand this tosh. Words and phrases in the text like 'of course' and 'therefore' have a spurious sounding logic to them, as if only idiots could fail to understand the elegance of the thesis. I have to keep looking in the mirror and saying: 'No, you are not crazy, you are simply suffering from *folie à deux*, the condition whereby sane people think they are mad if they live long enough with someone who actually is.' Even Einstein would take one look at this stuff, cry 'Bollocks', and throw it in the bin, before retiring to do something fulfilling, like copying out the telephone directory.

However, my favourite in this particular pack was the story on page B5.6 about a girl described as having 'moderate learning difficulties' who was only given a W for the following, and I swear I have made none of this up. I quote directly again: 'When the child was presented with Ma3 Pupil Sheet 1, the teacher tried to encourage her to sit on a chair, but she preferred to sit under the table. Eventually, she was persuaded out from under the table and she drew round her hand. In the story-writing session she listened to the teacher's introduction with her classmates and then the teacher tried to encourage her to write 'shoe'. She preferred to run around the class with the shoe. In the end the teacher wrote 'shoe' in dots and the child joined them up.'

I have news for you, SEAC. We are not talking 'moderate learning difficulties' here, we are talking genius. Give her level 10 for insight and have done with it. What we are witnessing is the most insightful comment on the whole assessment exercise so far — run round the room clutching your shoe and hide under the table. It says it all, economically, unambiguously.

The other explanation, *of course*, to crib a SEAC cliché, is that the 'she' in question was not a pupil at all, but rather the head of the school undergoing an acute attack of Mad Curriculum Disease.

So, if you see any teachers or heads hiding under tables, drawing round their hand for no apparent reason, or running round the room brandishing a piece of footwear, blathering 'there was an old woman who lived in a shoe', then just phone the local Mad Curriculum Disease isolation hospital, for these are the classic symptoms of the ailment. Then ring SEAC and tell them the story so they can include it in next year's true blue instruction manual.

Times Educational Supplement 8.1.93

Bad language and the wages of syntax

It is a great pity that the teaching of English has not only become controversial, but has been made such a political issue. Successive ministers have stigmatised English teachers as wild subversives, eager to bury our national language, rather than enhance it, and press reports of the national curriculum proposals in English were so inaccurate and hysterical that the chairman of the working group had to write his own book, *Cox on Cox,* to put the record straight. Indeed, both press and politicians gave the public the impression that a third of seven- year-olds could not even recognise three letters of the alphabet, when the true figure was just 1 or 2 per cent.

Why is there such a strong desire to believe that English teachers, the very people charged with extending and sustaining literacy, should want to create a nation of illiterates? After all, undertakers, who spend their professional lives waiting for you to snuff it so that they can inter or incinerate you, get a fairly cheerful press by comparison, and rarely are science teachers accused of wanting to blow children up or dissolve them. Even the former Prime Minister could not resist hammering English teachers, and, although Snow White has now departed, this has not prevented the seven dwarfs from carrying on the good work.

Yet many teachers have worked hard to encourage children to enjoy reading from an early age, to write for different audiences and for specific purposes, and to develop the confidence to speak clearly about a variety of topics, as well as to listen to others. I know that my own son has a much better sense of audience and register than I had at his age, and he wrote more than 60 pieces of work during his GCSE course, much more than I did at the same stage for O-level.

Wittgenstein said that 'the limits of my language mean the limits of my world', and the explanation for English teachers' bad press might be that, since language is so vital in modern life, there is a sense of desperation that the next generation might not acquire sufficient competence to survive and flourish. In the same way that young children terrorise themselves with nightmares about ghosts and bogeymen, we perhaps like to be frightened with fantasies that Standard English is going to the dogs, and that English teachers are the instigators of its demise.

Yet language is dynamic and changing. If you knock on the door of a member of your family and are asked, 'Who is it?', do you reply 'It is I'? I should be surprised if Kenneth Clarke does, but he always tries to give the impression that he was the guardian of traditional language, as do other politicians who daily mangle it. John Patten has already got into the act by suggesting that new English tests for 14-year-olds, which will concentrate on grammar and Shakespeare, will restore 'real education'. I am sure that the fact that 'The Campaign for Real Education' is the name of one of the more vociferous right- wing pressure groups had completely escaped his notice.

However, I am delighted he decided to junk all the other kinds of test for 14-year-olds, even if this was the equivalent of flushing a few million pounds of public cash down the toilet, and go for these new back-to-basic shorties instead, because my own consortium, the Forsooth Gadzooks Perchance Traditional English Testing Company Plc, has just won the contract to produce next year's English tests for 14-year-olds, I am working on the items at this very moment.

1. In 1596 Shakespeare wrote a play entitled *The Merchant of*:
   a) Venice (b) Verona (c) Skegness

2. King Lear's youngest daughter was called:
   (a)Cordelia (b) Gonerilandregan (c) Kylie

3. When Macbeth said, 'Is this a dagger which I see before me, the handle toward my hand?', was he:
   (a) contemplating murder (b) contemplating his navel (c) pissed out of his skull

4. In *The Merchant of Skegness,* when Portia says, 'I know it is a sin to be a mocker: but he! why, he hath a horse better than Neapolitan's; a better bad habit of frowning than the Count Palatine: he is every man in no man; if a throstle sing, he falls straight a-capering,' what the hell is she on about?

5. Which of the following is true:

   (a) *As You Like It* is a Shakespeare play

   (b) *Like It Or Lump It* is the title of the next White Paper on education

    (c)   *As You Lick It* is a play about a minister and the Prime Minister's left boot

6.   What do we call the verbal noun, as in 'He enjoys walking':

    (a)   a gerund

    (b)   a gerundive

    (c)   Gerald

7.   Underline each instance of pluperfect tense in the following sentence: 'When the English teacher had received the letter telling him what the minister had decided about English testing, he had realised that he had been had.'

8.   Which of these sentences is correct:

    (a)   Poor grammar often leads to bad use of language

    (b)   Poor grandma often uses bad language

    (c)   Syntax is what the Government levies on beer and cigarettes

9.   Write a short essay on either 'A day in the life of a penny', or 'The things what I have learned about Shakespeare and grammar through doing this 14-plus exam'.

10.   'Politicians being potty...' is

    (a)   a phrase

    (b)   a clause

    (c)   an inescapable fact of life.

Times Educational Supplement 10.7.92

Government anthology key stage 3

All pupils at all tiers (or is it 'tears'?), must study the contents of this anthology for the key stage 3 test in English on Wednesday June 9, 1993, starting at 9.30am. The test will be designed to assess pupils' knowledge and understanding of the texts in this official Government anthology of great literature for 14-year-olds. The time allowed for the test will be 15 minutes or whenever the candidate walks out in disgust, whichever is sooner.

I. Compulsory Shakespeare
Julius Caesar (for 14-year-olds)
Brute and Cass are pals, Jules is bad. He has a big head. Brute and Cass say, 'Jules is a bad lad. He has a big head. Let us do him in'. They stab him. Jules says, 'You too Brute, then die Jules'. He dies. Mark Tony comes in. Mark Tony is big. He is a pal of Cleo (in another play by Will). He says, 'Pals, lend me your ears'. They all fight. Brute and Cass both die. Mark Tony wins, so he can be in another play by Will called *Tony and Cleo* (set book next year).

Sample questions:

1.   Who are pals?

2.   Name two things that are big.

3.   Will is (tick one answer) (a) boring (b) a simpleton (c) turning in his grave.

Answers:

1.   Brute and Cass, Tony and Cleo, Tony and everybody (3 marks)

2.   Mark Tony, Jules's head (2 marks)

3.   (c) (level 10 for correct answer)

II. Other Writers

A.   Very Old

Geoff Chaucer was a man who lived a long time ago. He spoke funny English, though people didn't think it was funny at the time. He went with 28 other pilgrims to Canterbury (that's in Kent, see geography paper). As the Channel tunnel link hadn't been built, it took him and his pals a long time, so they told each other stories, as people do when they're stuck in a train. The best ones are the stories told by the Miller and the Reeve. They're really rude (too much bonking, so we can't include them in the anthology — sorry!). We don't want to bore you with the whole lot, but here's a bit to give you the idea.

> Whan that Aprill with her shoures soote
> The droghte of March hat perced to the roote,
> And bathed every veyne in swich licour
> Of which vertu engendred is the flour;

Basically this means 'Once its stopped peeing it down, the flowers grow'.

Sample questions:

1.   How many pilgrims were there? (don't forget to include Geoff himself!)

2.   Did it rain when Geoff was alive?

B.   Oldish

Ode to various birds by Shelley N. Keats (at least 100 years ago)

> Hail to thee, blithe spirit!
> Skylark thou never wert —
> Away! Away! for I will fly to thee,
> Oh nightingale, and any other birds,
> Like sparrows and that sort of thing.

Learn these names of writers off by heart: Coleridge, Swift, Pope, Brontë (don't forget the two dots over the letter 'e', or you'll lose marks!), Goldsmith, Byron, Swift, Tennyson, Xenophon de Montfort Cressigny-Fforbes-Ffrench.

Sample questions:

1.   Name three birds

2. Which of the names above is not a writer, but has been made up just so that you can learn a long name and impress everybody (it's good training for your memory, honest!)

C. Modern writers no one's ever heard of

The lawn mower by U.T.T.R. Nonentity, died (we think) about 1960-ish.

> I hear a bee,
> Or is it a lawn mower?
> It might be an Atco,
> Or even a Flymo.

Sample questions:

1. Name two makes of lawn mower.
2. What kind of prat can't tell a bee from a lawn mower? (Answer, U.T.T.R. Nonentity)

D. Contemporary Poem

> I wrote this poem in thirty secs.
> And no one's ever heard of me.
> It doesn't scan and there's no sex,
> So put it in your anthologee.
> (*Ted Wragg, 1993*)

Times Educational Supplement 22.1.93

Ruled by the free market Stalinists

When John Patten used the word 'Neanderthal' to describe the views of parents who had been turned away without gaining an audience with the great man, it neatly summed up the contemptuous attitude of the Government towards anyone daring to make a suggestion about its educational policies. Representatives of parent-teacher associations from England, Scotland and Wales had gathered eagerly at the House of Commons, hoping to achieve something few bird-watchers have managed recently, a rare sighting of the species *Pattenus minimus*, a distant cousin of the great tit. They were shown the door.

Members of PTAs put in hours raising money for schools, organising events, buying books and equipment. Yet Bouffant Boy could not spare a few moments to talk to these parents' representatives, although he could find time to go on BBC Radio and rubbish them. What arrogance. When asked to face his critics, he shows all the bravura of a Trappist monk, but in the safe privacy of a radio studio he becomes Wild Bill Hickok.

I received a letter from some Russians who had been studying British education. They described our present system as 'Stalinist'. It has come to something when those who have savoured at first hand the effects of an authoritarian, tightly controlled, bureaucratic centralist state, with party placemen in key positions and no voice for opposing views, tell us that this is what we now have.

Governments should not even attempt to run 25,000 schools, as the chaos of the past few years reveals. Authoritarianism is the only resort. First make 25,000 schools, in theory, autonomous businesses, each with a managing director and a board of directors. Then create divisions, school against school, parent against parent in competition for places, heads against teachers, pupil against pupil in the testing race, schools against LEAs. Finally impose hundreds of directives on teachers about curriculum, management, assessment. when they protest, ignore them. If they try to rebel, crush them.

Take the whole issue of national testing. What will happen if schools go ahead with their proposed boycott? There have been threats about breach of contract and docking of salary, despite the apparent autonomy of these 25,000 small businesses. Will the police question heads? ('Allo, 'allo', 'allo. Who's been a naughty boy then?') Or will the Government send in the Army, with the 2nd Paras marking this year's SATs? ('ere, Sarge, what's a bleedin' vector?').

One essential feature of central control is a dense, labyrinthine bureaucracy that saps the energy of those under its heel. This Kafka nightmare has been nowhere better fulfilled than in the Scilly Isles. These tiny civilised islands came top of the national examinations league last summer, so the market philosophy decrees that the parents of the nation's 8,000,000 schoolchildren should now desert their 25,000 mainland schools and catch the next boat across, leaving 25,000 bankrupt schools behind them. Well, that's the market for you, the strong win and the weak go to the wall.

It must have been in anticipation of this huge exodus that the Government's wise agency sent a recent mailing of key stage 1 SATs to the Scilly Isles. Just listen to this for a prime argument against state control of education. There are only 32 Year 2 children in the Scilly Isles. For just one subject they have been sent 4,000 tests in 40 boxes, enough for more than 100 copies per child. One small school was sent 14 teacher packs. Worse, this huge mailing was accompanied by customs clearance documents, as if the Scilly Isles were some foreign country. Stalin must be chuckling in his grave. If Franz Kafka had written up the story, his publisher would have told him it was too far fetched.

One of the features of a monolithic state system is that it is usually built on one person's vision. We are told nowadays that John Major really runs education, that his philosophy, such as it is, derives from a tiny circle of right-wing advisers, and that Bouffant Boy is just his glove puppet. Curious to know what this prime ministerial vision for education might be, I turned in eagerly to his party-political broadcast. When it came it was worth waiting for. What he wanted, he told us, was for children to read, write, and add up.

So that was his vision. Two thoughts occurred to me immediately. First of all, is there, anyone in Britain who *doesn't* want children to learn to read, or write, or add? If so bring this lunatic forward and let's have a public hanging. Second, is that it? Just add-up sums, not a single take-away, share-by or times? A bit of a slim curriculum, isn't it? I've heard of back to basics, but even the Neanderthals must have ventured beyond this inchoate simplicity.

Small wonder that teaching is becoming so de-professionalised. Any fool can do it. The Government tells teachers what to teach, and increasingly how to teach it. Whereas in most professions experience and expertise are highly valued and rewarded, in teaching you have to look over your shoulder when you reach the top of the scale or obtain a senior post, in case hard-up governors have to fire you and bring in a novice to save money. It is the only professional ladder to consist of a few rungs and an abyss.

Nor is it any surprise, from well-ordered Downing Street leaks, that Mr Major's view of teacher training, shortly to be announced to an astonished world, is to bung them straight into schools (despite the massive scandal in the press whenever a school has hired an untrained unqualified youngster) and cut out all that fancy higher education bit, especially for key stage 1 teachers. In Mr Major's 'plain man' view, mothers can teach in primary schools with one year's training. Simple. That's the trouble with a centralist system dependent on the vision of one man.

Times Educational Supplement 5.2.93

Must Paul be written off?

I remember Paul well. Before the national curriculum was formally introduced, I spent a term teaching several of the proposed science topics to a class of seven-year-olds, and he was a pupil in it. The school was in what used to be called a 'social priority area', when downtown schools were places that society tried to help. Nowadays they are regarded as rat holes which need a squad of retired heads to sort them out.

Paul was one of those lads who could easily be labelled 'thick'. He was a good-natured boy of few words. His general strategy was to shrug his shoulders and reply 'Dunno,' to almost any question. When we finished the term's work I devised an oral test of what had been learned. Paul's opening reply to each question was his usual 'Search me' response. Yet he had understood the whole term's work almost perfectly, of that I have no doubt, functioning at level 2 or 3.

Take for example his reply to my question about magnets and magnetism. The average seven-year-old is expected to know that magnets pick up some things but not others. When I showed Paul a magnet, his initial response was to say that he could not tell me anything about it. Several minutes later, with no clues from me other than a constant urging to try hard, think carefully, recall what we had done, he told me the following: that magnets pick up some things but not others; that they do not pick up all metals not brass, not copper, not aluminium (he struggled with the name), but just 'things what's got iron in them' (marks deducted for ungrammatical English); that a magnet picks up a tin-can lid 'because it's got some iron in it as well'; that north sticks to south and south to north, but that the other way round two magnets push each other away.

I tell this story because Lord Griffiths of Fforestfach, chairman of the School Examinations and Assessment Council, says that teacher assessment is 'not as reliable or as publicly credible as a formal written test taken simultaneously by all pupils under controlled conditions'. That's Ffuny. I have a Ffair Ffirst-hand knowledge of many Fforms of Fformal and inFformal testing, so I Ffind it Ffaintly Ffoolish, nay Ffarcical, to Ffeel I must have Ffull Ffaith in written Ttests, sorry, tests.

On any written test about magnets and magnetism Paul would be lucky to get a level 1. In the restricted sense in which the world 'reliability' is used in the argot of assessment, such a written test would indeed be 'reliable'. Paul and thousands of streetwise city children like him, would all get, at best, a level 1 on version A of the test and, a week later, secure a level 1 on version B of the test. Split it in half and they would get level 1 on the even-numbered questions and level 1 on the odd-numbered questions. Give it to several different markers, all operating independently of each other, and again level 1 will be the outcome. In the limited terms of a pencil-and-paper test Paul is indubitably level. 1. He and the other thousands can all be 'reliably' league-tabled across the nation.

What is wrong with the searing and self-fulfilling logic of this line of argument about test reliability, however, is that it ignores the parallel concept of 'validity'. A test is valid in so far as it measures what it purports to measure.

There are many children whose abilities, insights and understanding are not accurately measured by pencil and paper tests. Smart teachers, however, spot and encourage their talents. Some children are capable of intelligent action, but less good at writing it down; some are streetwise, but appear inept in school, some talk freely, but find their brains turn to concrete at the sight of printed sheets. The best-known written test failures become millionaire entrepreneurs, prime ministers, or go on to success in the arts or other forms of expression.

Before the first SATs, ministers put out the propaganda that written tests were necessary because they were rigorous, and that teachers would be too soft in their assessments. When it turned out the teachers' grades were slightly *lower* than written test scores, they maintained their attack on teachers by trying to set parents against them. Instead of saying that the tests may have been too easy, they suggested that teachers were not recognising children's true talents. It is a dirty game.

When will they recognise that sensible assessment involves a mixture of methods, none in itself necessarily superior, just different according to the circumstances. The Royal Society laments the attack on coursework, because it recognises that certain aspects of maths and science are not measured especially well in the exam room. Putting a premium on written tests, while discrediting other forms of assessment, is like saying that the only proper record of someone's wedding is the newspaper feature. Forget the photographs, the video, personal memories, oral accounts, wedding presents, participants' perceptions.

I have a fancy to apply this monochrome vision more widely. Perhaps Paul Gascoigne could be judged on the results of a written test on how to play football. Richard Branson could be given an hour to write an essay entitled 'How to make money'. Why do we listen to Pavarotti? Could we not rather assess his talent by reading his definition of a crotchet, written, of course, under strict exam conditions, or his explanation of the word *andante?* And is John Major fully summed up by his two O-levels? You have exactly 40 minutes to reply, no conferring.

Human judgement may be Ffrail, it may not be entirely Ffaultless, but it should play a Ffull part, alongside other Fforms of assessment, in the appraisal of progress and potential. It is Ffolly Ffor SEAC to insist that only the exam room reveals all. What a Fflimsy Ffoundation. Fffffrightening.

Times Educational Supplement 19.2.93

Don't put a moral lead on our necks

To read some of the pronouncements of politicians about schools teaching children right and wrong, you would think no primary and secondary school had ever tried personal, social and moral education. The suggestion seems to be that teachers have not really spotted this one and needed it pointing out. Presumably the conversation would go:

> *Politician:* I think schools should teach children what is right and wrong.

> *Teacher* That's a very good point, squire. I'm most grateful. As head of the Department of Shoplifting and Car Theft I'll raise that at the next staff meeting, because no one has ever thought of it before in the entire history of the school.

Has no one taken the trouble to ask about all the work that has been done for years in tutor groups, assemblies, RE lessons, or in context whenever children transgress? Is the assumption that no teacher has ever bothered, or that doing wrong is condoned, perhaps even taught? It is another oblique slight, a further piece of sly innuendo that assigns blame for society's ills to teachers and diminishes the profession in the eyes of the public.

What about all those highly moral stories in the primary school where villains come to grief, the sessions on moral dilemmas in secondary schools, the harangues in assembly? The average pupil probably feels moralised to death, rather than urged to commit evil. It is supposed to be one of the reasons why the marginally motivated switch off schooling. Teachers are normally thought to be narrow-minded prigs who frown on naughtiness and go round shouting at children who misbehave. Did I miss something? Have they all suddenly been transformed into Fagin?

Old Fagin would probably do quite well in the present education climate. He would almost certainly get a performance-related bonus as he seemed to be doing all the things the Government wants: he had little or no truancy, he had opted out of his LEA, his overheads were low, he was good at raising extra cash and was no drain on the public purse because he picked the private one, there was a thriving vocational education programme, and he dealt firmly with discipline problems.

In the attainment targets of the national curriculum syllabus for crime he must come very high in the league table. I wonder what the SATs were like — Level 3, pick someone's pocket and run away: Level 6, pick someone's pocket and not have to run away because he never noticed; Level 10, pick someone's pocket and get paid for it as well by becoming an accountant.

Perhaps this is the perception of those politicians who seem to believe that teachers do not give a fig for what is right or wrong. I remember a former Home Secretary being interviewed after a bout of urban riots. When asked for the possible causes, he replied: 'I think we need look no further than our schools.' In the fevered imagination of those who make these unfounded assertions there may indeed be a belief that the average secondary school time-table starts with shoplifting first period, goes on to a double lesson of safe-cracking, followed by a practical workshop session on breaking and entering, and ends with a project on armed robbery. No wonder coursework is so unpopular with ministers.

If schools are indeed nurseries for crime this raises interesting issues about inspection. Presumably the Office for Standards in Education would have to seek active and successful criminals as registered inspectors. Those one-week training courses they run in hotels could be hilarious. I can just see the clientele: a room full of shifty-looking masked men with cauliflower ears and broken noses in striped jerseys, clutching jemmies and bags marked 'Swag', glancing furtively over their shoulders and nicking the silver when no one is looking — a bit like a Cabinet meeting.

Then there would be the paradox of lay inspectors. Since the prime qualification for being a lay inspector is to know absolutely bog all about the matter in hand, teachers themselves could sign up. 'But I know nothing at all about crime,' 'Welcome aboard friend, just what we're looking for.'

This notion that schools are breeding grounds for crime may explain the recent tradition of links between the Home Office and the Department for Education. John Patten came from the Home Office, Kenneth Baker and Kenneth Clarke moved to it, all in the interest of continuity presumably. It may also explain why the police are now complaining about being buried under bureaucracy and having no time to fight crime. Suspicion and mistrust breed bureaucracy, as ministers impose it punitively on those they feel they dare not let out of their sight.

But if teachers are really as incompetent as ministers like to make out, then surely the solution is to put crime fairly and squarely into the national curriculum. Then, according to ministers' own judgement, teachers would teach it so badly that thousands of school-leavers would be below average at it. They would walk into banks with their masks on back to front, steal Reliant Robins as their getaway cars, kidnap unpopular people that nobody wanted back anyway, and sign their name and address on the bottom of their ransom-demand notes. Britain would sink to the bottom of the international crime league table. It would be a brilliant solution to the appalling rise in crime in recent years.

The sad truth of the matter, however, is that attacking schools and teachers on the morality ticket is a convenient way of distracting attention from the Government's own failures, with the added bonus of keeping the profession pegged at a low level of public esteem and therefore impotent. The Government has had more than a few scandals of its own, and some of its members have not exactly been pillars of rectitude, either in their private life or their political dealings. If a moral lead is needed, then they should lay off attacking the very people whose daily job involves giving one and stop to look in the mirror occasionally.

Times Educational Supplement 2.4.93

The sooner you spot where he's falling down the sooner you can lend a hand

From quite early on in school life, your child starts to develop different levels of ability in different subjects; strengths that should be encouraged, so they continue to flourish; and weaknesses that must be addressed, if potential is to be fulfilled.

That is why children are being assessed at the ages of 7 and 14 and why we are spending £700,000 of public money to pretend there is no such thing as a teachers' boyc... (Ooops! nearly mentioned the 'B' word there).

The tests are simply designed to measure your child's progress against consistent, national standards, or at least that's what it says in the briefing notes we've been given by the Department for Education, so that everyone involved in his or her education has a clear view of how things are going — or would have, were it not for the teachers' boyc... (Drat! nearly said it again).

Even if your child is not doing the tests this year, it's important that you understand how they work, or rather don't work, given the teachers' boyc... (Damn! I must stop doing that).

So a free parent's guide, *Why We're Wasting £700,000 of Public Money on This Kind of Advertising Crap,* has been produced to hoodwink...er, I mean, to inform you about this year's tests without ever mentioning the teachers' boyc... (Aaaargh!).

Meanwhile, this advert will insult you with a few weary education clichés about you needing to 'do your homework', so you can help your child 'pull up his socks', and 'get to the top of the class'. It's as easy as ABC, so send for the guide now, or you'll have to put on your dunce's cap and stand in the corner.

It you want more information about... (What's that? Another adviser from the School Examinations and Assessment Council has resigned? Are any of the buggers left? Oh well, I suppose that's something else we mustn't mention)... anyway, if you really want a copy of this expensive public relations tosh, then call Mr Loonytunes at the DFE, or write to *Loonytunes, DFE, Costa Bomb, Biggar, Berks.*

You know it makes sense.

Times Educational Supplement 14.5.93

BETTER BILGE FROM BIGGER BUDGETS

It's Tee Hee Hee, with the DFE

Tick box(es) for a copy of *Why We're Wasting £700,000 of Public Money on This Kind of Advertising Crap.*

I can read SEAC literature, so I would like this leaflet in:

Double Dutch ❑ Sanskrit ❑ Linear B ❑ Bakerspeak ❑

I would like to receive future DFE leaflets for parents:

ready perforated ❑ mixed with compost ❑ only after my death ❑

I am a: Neanderthal ❑ Cro-Magnon ❑ dinosaur ❑

NAME _____

ADDRESS _____

_____

DFE: DEAD FROM EXHAUSTION

Exclusive — those tests in full

1993 Standard Assessment Tasks — Key Stage 3

Invigilation. At least two invigilators should be provided for each session. Both should wear the official armbands provided, the more senior the one marked *Obergauleiter*, the more junior the one labelled *Untergauleiter*. Invigilators should prowl round the room in a slightly sinister low crouch, the way teachers used to in the good old days when we had O-levels, and bark: 'Are you cribbing boy?' at any pupils who appear to be cheating.

English
1. Shakespeare for 14-year-olds

(a) Look at the two pictures provided in the brown envelope. They depict two scenes from your government set book *Julius Caesar for 14-year-olds*. Picture A shows Cassius talking to Brutus, saying 'Jules is bad. Let us do him in.' Picture B shows Brutus and Cassius standing over Caesar's dead body saying: 'Jules was bad, so we did him in.' Put the two pictures in the correct order in which they appear in the play.

(b) Imagine you are Jules. Out of the three statements below, tick the *two* remarks you are most likely to have made at the end of the play:

   (i)   'It's nice to have a few friends round.'

   (ii) 'Who the hell stuck this bloody great dagger in my ribs?'

   (iii) 'I am dead.'

(c) Tick whichever of the following Shakespeare play titles you feel describe this year's SATs: *As You Like It, Much Ado About Nothing, Measure for Measure, All's Well That Ends Well, The Tempest, The Comedy of Errors.*

2. Government Anthology of Very Short Extracts From Great English Literature. Write **True** or **False** against the two statements below.

(a)   Chaucer was an Arsenal supporter.

(b)   *Rasselas* is completely incomprehensible to most 14-year-olds.

3. Language. Put the following three statements into the correct order:

(a)   This year's SATs for 14-year-olds

(b)   complete farce, because the tests are stupid and most pupils are not actually doing them

(c)   are a

4. Spelling. Put a ring round any spelling mistakes in the following sentence: This examination room is completely emtpy, because instead of taking the test pupils are sitting in normal lessons learning soemthing useful.

Science

Take the rubber ball, squash ball and table tennis ball provided. Design an experiment to see which bounces highest. Write **True** or **False** against each of the statements below:

(a)   Our school should bounce to the top of the league, because no one else is doing the SATs.

(b)   This whole thing is a lot of balls.

Maths

(a)   Compile a league table of the SATs scores for the three schools A. B and C below. (N = the number of 14-year-old pupils on roll, E = the number of pupils who actually entered the examination, AL = the average national curriculum level obtained by the pupils). Your league table should place the school with the highest average level (AL) at the top and the one with the lowest AL at the bottom.

	N	E	AL
School A	120	0	0.00
School B	240	0	0.00
School C	180	0	0.00

(b)   If a government wastes £10,000,000 on SATs that no one actually does, and £700,000 on a campaign to send pamphlets to parents explaining about assessment, which are already out of date before they have even been mailed out, how much public money, to the nearest million pounds, has it wasted altogether?

Technology
Design a cockup
(a)   Plan a council that is responsible for both school curriculum and examinations. Then split it in two and put one half in London and the other in York. Bring the two halves back together again in London. Tell people it is a good idea.

(b)   Set up 25,000 schools and 450,000 teachers. Tell schools that anyone can teach, even if unqualified. Abandon your responsibility for training teachers. Leave schools to find their own teachers and train them themselves. Watch higher education collapse. Wait for large numbers of teachers to leave the profession when the graduate employment market improves. Laugh like a drain. Evaluate your cock-up.

Times Educational Supplement 28.5.93

There's no knowing where we're going

'Oh hellow, it's Scroggins here, *Daily Bugle*. I wonder if you can help me. I'm doing this feature on education today, and I just wanted to ask your opinion about something. Do you think knowledge is important?'

It was the sort of question that can easily pole-axe you at the end of the day. Was I supposed to say, 'Oh no, squire, no importance what-soever'? What passes for debate on education nowadays tends to press people into ludicrously unreal stereotypes — are you in favour of real books or phonics? Traditional or progressive teaching? Fish or chips? Jelly or custard? A knife or a fork? Are you a complete loony of this persuasion or an equally crazy disciple of that one?

It was tempting to reply, 'Of course I'm in favour of knowledge, you prat,' but that would probably count as a 'Don't know' in the *Bugle*. 'I love knowledge,' I went on. Ever since I eagerly culled the 'Did you know?' column of the *Wizard*, or whichever childhood comic had those fascinating facts about how often the Old Faithful geyser erupts in Yellowstone National Park — every 33 to 96 minutes — I have collected knowledge avidly.

But why, in this crude debate, is knowledge seen as the opposite of understanding? The pretence is that there are two groups of teachers; those who only peddle knowledge and don't give a damn about under-standing, and their sworn enemies who do the exact opposite.

The other fantasy, spread by right-wing pressure groups, is that there is no knowledge in the national curriculum.

That the national curriculum has been dry-cleaned of any significant content is one of the sicker jokes put around by some of the ranting think-tanks. I can only assume they have never fondled the many pages of the national curriculum history document, for example. Had they flicked idly through its prolix text, their eyes might just have picked out a few of the numerous topics to be studied by 7 to 11-year-olds at key stage 2, such as the Egyptians, the Greeks, the Romans, the Anglo-Saxons, the Vikings, the Aztecs, the Tudors and the Stuarts, and the Victorians.

Far from being starved of knowledge, primary pupils are supposed to be drowned in it. There is so much to cover that no one can hope to do more than scratch the surface. The history programme is full of grand sweeps, such as 'changes in land transport in prehistoric, Roman and Victorian times' — just a few years to talk about there. When describing such topics as 'food and farming' and 'ships and sea-farers' the instructions say 'this unit should cover a timespan of at least a thousand years' and 'show links between local, British, European and world history'.

Did anyone stop to work out what this mad rush through the knowledge of several millennia actually means in classroom terms? A thousand years of this and five hundred years of the other, given the relatively slight amount of time available for history compared with the core subjects, allows a couple of minutes for each year. It's a tough life for the pupils. Sneeze, and you miss the Spanish Armada. Nip off to the loo, and when you return the Second World War is over. Go down with flu, and its goodbye to the history of transport before and after the wheel.

All of this is bad news for John Major's army of barely-trained mums, who are soon to swell the ranks of the teaching profession when graduate status is no longer required. What with Dad's Army doing the lay inspection of schools and Mum's Army carrying out the teaching, it is nice to know that amateurism is alive and well. Neither group will be awash with knowledge.

Presumably, when Auntie Mavis goes to sign up as one of these new-style cheapie, instant teachers, she will, like the lay inspectors, be sent away on a one-week course in a hotel to learn all there is to know about teaching. 'Right ladies, welcome to the Mum's Army teacher training course. Now, we'll be doing the Aztecs at 9.30, a thousand years of plough design at 9.35, the history of transport before and after the wheel at 9.40, all the invaders and settlers from the beginning of time to the present day at 9.45, and then we'll move on to maths, science and technology before coffee. This afternoon it's class management, questioning and explaining, disruptive pupils, assessment and how to handle group work.'

In fact, why bother? Just tell Auntie Mavis to get her John Major teaching certificate from the chap by the door straight-away, grab her SAT pack from the pile at the back, and she can start teaching Year 2 this afternoon. The secondary people can stay behind for a couple of minutes to collect their DFE leaflets on how to teach GCSE in two easy steps.

So, are we serious about knowledge nor not? The Mum's Army idea is predicated on the assumption that little children don't know too much, so their teachers don't need any fancy knowledge themselves of the nine subjects of the national curriculum or of the craft skills of the profession.

It is as if the medical profession were to be told that paediatricians could in future be mums, since they have had children, and that they would only need a week in a hotel to clue them in about measles, whooping cough and nappy rash.

But why confine the idea to mums? If the John Major quickie badge is available to anyone with arguably relevant experience, then I would recruit an army of sewage workers to the teaching profession. At least they would be well used to handling all the crap that teachers have to put up with nowadays.

Times Educational Supplement 11.6.93

Peace in the civil English war

If you were to believe everything you read in some of the popular press, you could be forgiven for thinking that English teachers were locked in mortal combat.

It would appear, from these accounts, that primary teachers are divided into trendy purveyors of something called the 'real books' method, whereby children are sent to the school library in the faint hope that they will teach themselves to read, and good old traditionalists who have them chant 'c-a-t equals cat'. Secondary school English teachers are supposed to belong either to the 'I don't give a fig about spelling and punctuation' club, or the 'Bring back Coleridge' faction.

There is, indeed, a lively debate about how to teach English, but most teachers use a mixture of approaches. When Her Majesty's Inspectorate conducted a survey of the teaching of reading in primary schools earlier this year, far from finding two camps of ideological fanatics, they discovered that only 5 per cent of primary teachers used exclusively the 'real books' approach, which eschews structured reading schemes, and only 3 per cent favoured a phonics-only style of teaching.

The vast majority varied what they did according to the individual child's needs and the context in which reading occurred. Indeed, some of the poorest reading achievement was recorded in classrooms where only one method was adopted, be it 'real books' or phonics.

One of the problems with public and press reaction to teaching methods is that the first filtering of reports and National Curriculum documents is often done by right-wing pressure groups. Their denunciations sometimes receive more publicity than the original reports. When the National Curriculum proposals for English were first published, the then Prime Minister, Margaret Thatcher, let it be known that she was displeased. Her criticisms about lack of attention to grammar were close to those of the Centre for Policy Studies, the right-wing think tank which she and Lord Joseph had established.

Professor Brian Cox, who had chaired the English working group which had framed the recommendations, subsequently had to write letters to the press pointing out the sections of the report which listed grammatical terms and constructs that children were expected to know. He also had to dispel the mistaken notion that English teachers were set to abandon standard English.

The National Curriculum document strongly supported the teaching of standard English as a foundation stone of children's learning and ultimate prosperity. It was about received pronunciation, not standard English, that the report was flexible, pointing out that many children have some kind of regional accent or stock of dialect words and phrases, and that this should not be ridiculed.

English teachers are asked to cover a wide spectrum. In addition to the fundamentals of reading, writing, listening, speaking and spelling required by the National Curriculum, they usually teach drama and media studies and are expected to show greater interest in the whole child than many other subject specialists. Most children probably write more prose, and certainly compose more poetry, in school than many of their parents. Hence the *joke:* 'Don't look out of the window or she'll make you write a poem about it.'

Both science and English are important subjects in the curriculum, but if something goes amiss in adult life, then it is more likely that blame will be attached to English teachers than to science teachers.

In the Sixties, Andrew Wilkinson drew attention to this wide role when he described several models of English teaching, ranging from 'proof reader', which involved meticulous correction of every spelling and punctuation error, to 'Grendel's mother, guardian of the word-hoard', the person with the awesome responsibility of keeping alive and enhancing the nation's cultural heritage.

Fortunately, English teachers are among the best qualified academically to undertake such an assignment. Analysis of graduate recruits to teaching shows that English, history and modern languages entrants have more firsts and upper seconds than in any other subject. English and history teachers frequently go on to take senior positions in secondary schools as heads and deputies. They are also among the best organised teachers professionally. Many belong to the National Association of Teachers of English (Nate) which, through its numerous conferences and publications, exercises a greater influence on its members than most comparable subject groups.

The major language and literacy issues affect English teaching at all stages of education, albeit in different ways. In primary schools, all teachers are expected to be English teachers, even if the school has specific language or reading specialists. A survey of more than 900 primary teachers which we undertook at Exeter University as part of the Leverhulme Primary Project showed that over 80 per cent expressed confidence in their ability to teach English effectively, compared with only one in three who felt equally competent in science and a mere one in seven in technology.

One noticeable trend in primary schools in recent years has been the tendency to see language as an integrated set of activities, rather than as separate skills divorced from each other. One popular reading scheme, Breakthrough to Literacy, which was developed in the Sixties, used an initial stock of 200 common words on which the early years story books were based. Children were also given a 'sentence maker', a Scrabble-type stand on which they could assemble their own sentences using the same list and adding fresh words as their vocabulary developed. Thus reading, writing and speaking could be linked together.

In secondary schools, English teachers have been in short supply in recent years, even though the subject never used to appear on official shortage lists. Schools usually covered the gaps by asking teachers not qualified in English to take classes. The not-so-funny joke was that anyone could teach English.

It is quite legitimate, of course, to say that all teachers are, to some extent, teachers of English. When the term 'inversely proportional' occurs in a lesson dealing with a law in physics, it would be pointless for the teacher to ask children to wait until the English specialist had time to explain the meaning to those who were not clear. Language is best learned in context.

However, the skills needed by a good secondary English teacher are formidable — a good grasp of both children's and adult literature, the ability to develop pupils' ability to write on a variety of topics for different audiences and to speak clearly and with confidence in public or private.

The nature of English teaching in both schools and colleges of further education has also come under scrutiny with the development of more vocational work in the 14 to 19 age range. The narrow instrumental view is that all that is needed is a quick course in gas fitters' English or whatever, a few lecturettes on how to spell 'radiator' and 'pipes'. Vocational literacy involves much more than this, and most teachers prefer a broader approach which, while covering the writing of technical reports or communicating with clients, will not neglect wider issues.

Dr Colin Harrison, of Nottingham University, has analysed some of the literacy demands in daily adult life. To read a tabloid newspaper, you need a reading age of about 12 or 13 (i.e. to be able to read as well as the average 12 or 13 year-old). A 'quality' newspaper like *The Observer* requires a reading age of 17 or 18. Some of the documents which people need to understand to obtain their rights or discharge their duties are even more exacting. A leaflet entitled 'How to Claim Your Free Glasses' was one of the most difficult analysed by Dr Harrison, so not only could these poor beggars not see, but even if they had been able to they may not, in many cases have been able to understand.

In the complex world of the late twentieth century, those without basic literacy can fall prey to the many predators in our society. It is a heavy responsibility that we impose on Grendel's mother.

Observer 22.9.91

Flying a kite for future technologists

'I don't like it. I don't like it. I don't like it at all.' Thus spake the former Prime Minister about the history national curriculum on the one occasion I met her, shaking her head violently. When I first read through the national curriculum technology syllabus I knew exactly how Mrs T must have felt, because I didn't like it one bit either. It was the way that design, technology, information technology, business studies and home economics had all been rammed together that put me off.

I am keen on cookery, so when I met one of the national curriculum technology gurus I asked why this vital subject had been buried in such a vast syllabus. 'Ah,' he said, 'cookery must be seen as a design challenge. First you design your beefburger, then you cook it, and finally you design a marketing strategy for it.' No wonder parents are complaining they don't get nice buns at parents' evenings, like they used to in the old days. Their kids are too busy designing bloody beefburgers, and if they do make buns they probably try to flog them for a profit nowadays.

However, there is no point in sitting around lamenting, so I decided to go and teach a bit of technology to a class of seven- year-olds at Bradley Rowe first school in Exeter. Green folder in one hand, bag full of goodies in the other, I entered the classroom with some trepidation. Like most primary teachers I would sooner wrestle with a boa constrictor than teach technology. As a child I was much happier playing football or reading a book than sweating over a hot Meccano set. Not for me a thousand hours making a model of the Forth Bridge that looked like a junk yard when finished.

When we surveyed more than 900 primary teachers as part of the Leverhulme primary project at Exeter University, only one in seven felt able to tackle technology without additional help. It was firmly bottom of the confidence league. So I was not the only person to go into catatonic shock when someone said, 'It's technology time'.

Actually, I have to say I loved it, but I cheated like mad. I got some great ideas from my colleague John Twyford, but it was frustrating trying to follow the green folder. According to the key stage 1 syllabus we should have been making things like bird scarers. Well, nuts to that. We made superb little kites out of two pieces of wood veneer strips, or a couple of art straws, and coloured tissue paper.

Most fun of all was making tortoises. You take that old favourite, the cotton reel with the two matchsticks at either end and an elastic band through the middle, which plods slowly along when you wind up the elastic. Then you get a circle of card, snip out a thin 'piece of pie' as one child called it, glue together, add a head and a tail, colour it brightly stick it over the wound-up cotton reel, and Bob's your tortoise. When one girl tightened up her elastic band before launching her little plodding beastie, and said 'I'm just putting some more energy into its motor', I was in ecstasy. There it was, science attainment target five under the new scheme of things. We had actually combined science and technology. The National Curriculum Council would be delirious with joy.

But I was left with many doubts. I cheated quite a bit by doing some 'design' exercises separately from making things. We designed hundreds of buttons on a chess-board-type grid.

You put all the possible shapes along the top and the various materials along the side, so that each square contains a different button — a round plastic one, a square metal, an oval-shaped bone button, and crazy ones like flower-shaped chocolate buttons (a seven-year-old had just invented the world's first edible button — feeling peckish on you way home? Just eat your buttons).

The quality of children's ideas was brilliant, but they far outstripped their ability to make artefacts. There were tears of frustration when some of them found that the tissue paper for their kites tore when they cut it, as seven-year-olds were not allowed sharp scissors, only the blunt, round ones.

So how much should I do for them when they get stuck? You can't give seven-year-olds a power drill or a Stanley knife, but their ideas often need them.

Furthermore, technology projects are enormously time- and energy-consuming if you are to do them properly, and you can spend an awful lot of time with one small group or individual. Stuff all that rhetoric about jam tarts being a design challenge and a business. At the end of my technology project I had just one word to say — 'Help!'

Times Educational Supplement 27.9.91

Stop the mad whirligig, I want to get off

The news that the national curriculum is to be simplified is a welcome relief. When the final report of the national curriculum history working party first appeared, I read out some of the topics in key stage 2 to an audience of 400 primary teachers who had not seen it. It was a Cook's tour of the invaders and settlers from the beginning of time to the last busload of American tourists, plough designers, pyramid and Parthenon builders, Tudors and Stuarts, Victorians, Aztecs and the grotesque 'history of transport before and after the wheel'.

The audience rolled in the aisles chortling 'he's a lad, making all this stuff up', until I pointed out it was no spoof and would soon be statutory, 'Hello Strangeways' for anyone who did not teach it, as it would become as optional as breathing. It summed up the mad whirligig that the national curriculum had become.

The whole thing is now so complex and prescriptive it is regarded with great dismay by people from other countries: 'You must be mad, we've got ours down to about 15 pages' (Swedish delegate at Council of Europe meeting); 'Why don't you let schools vary it, like we do?' (Danish delegate); 'Why do you have a nine-subject curriculum for five-year-olds?' (Austrian primary school inspector); 'We used to look up to you as the place we would like to go, now you are like the place we used to be' (Polish visitor).

Most countries can give you a single pamphlet containing their national curriculum. 'Here's a copy of our Bavarian *Lehrplan*', said a Munich head when I visited him, 'Have you brought a copy of yours?' I stifled my mirth at the thought of a pantechnicon of folders, ring binders and booklets, plus amendments, abandoned at Dover docks.

The two greatly needed elements are a manageable single document and stability, rather than monthly alterations. That plus the ending of political interference are vital for the health of a national curriculum, which must be dynamic and changing, but on nothing like the current scale.

A nine-subject curriculum for five-year-olds makes no sense. I would go for a big bash on literacy, supported by four other major fields. Until children can read and write there is no point in saddling them with nine academic subjects, plus RE.

There are three ingredients in any big push for early literacy. The first is the need for diversity and individuality, different approaches to reading, writing and speaking/listening related to what works for the individual child, not what some central committee or the Government decrees. As one report put it '... the most successful infant teachers have refused to follow fashion and commit themselves to any one method. They choose methods and books to fit the age, interest and ability of individual pupils'. No, that was not the HMI report or that of the Three Wise Men, but the Plowden report 25 years ago.

The second need is for good preliminary assessment of what is likely to work for each child. Third, English must be learned in context, with every opportunity being exploited to read, write and talk not just about fiction and children's literature, but all the aspects of the curriculum.

This broadly based and integrated view of literacy, therefore, would need to be supported by the other major domains of the curriculum: numeracy, the arts (including movement), the world around us and how the world works (including science and technology). These five domains should not be as prescribed as the present nine subjects, yet they can embrace the best of what has been achieved so far. They should also permit plenty of practical and topic/project work, as well as quite specific targeted subject work where appropriate.

The early stages of key stage 2 should continue the five domains above, but with a shift in balance. Literacy remains central, but not quite as predominant as in the earlier stage, and the other domains especially numeracy and the world and its workings, come into greater prominence. At age nine a move can be made toward more specific treatment of the separate subjects, with some specialist teaching.

Other than a one-sentence mention, the original discussion paper for the national curriculum virtually omitted children with special educational needs, including the very able. Slower learning children have to contemplate a ladder designed for others. Some could spend 10 years trying to get off level 1. We desperately need a *bespoke curriculum* for these children, an individually tailored plan of action for each one.

I would welcome the redesign of the national curriculum and its simplification. It has produced some gains, notably in the much better teaching of the physical sciences and technology in primary schools, but also numerous losses because of its overly tight and prescriptive nature, becoming a bureaucratic nightmare. Just reduce the detail and the prescription, free up some of the week, and this will help eliminate the obliquely insulting insinuation that teachers have no ideas of their own.

Times Educational Supplement 16.10.92

Give the GCSE more of a chance

'We recommend that examining boards strive to ensure that standards be kept as similar as possible: (a) between the various boards, (b) between the various subjects, (c) from one year to the next.'

No, that is not an extract from the report on GCSE by Her Majesty's Inspectors last month, gleefully trumpeted by its critics as evidence the exam itself is a failure.

It is, in fact, the conclusion of a parliamentary select committee to which I was specialist adviser 15 years ago. Our 1977 report on O-level and CSE examining was far more damning than anything the inspectors said about GCSE last month.

It is a pity that what is, in many ways, a successful new examination, should have been publicly and prematurely labelled a failure by politicians and right-wingers who never endorsed its aspirations in the first place.

When Lord Joseph decided to merge the O-level and CSE in the mid-Eighties, he wanted a different kind of exam for 16-year-olds. Most of us are used to the sort of exam where the 'pass' mark is fixed somewhere in the middle, and the candidates are spread in a bell-shaped curve with a few at the top and bottom and the majority around the centre, the 'norm-referenced' test.

The original intention of the GCSE was that it should be much more like the driving test, or gymnastics awards — if you have fulfilled the requirements for a particular grade then you get it, whether there are 2 per cent or 92 per cent at the same level, the 'criterion-referenced' approach to testing. The GCSE has not entirely shifted to this basis, but any move in that direction can change the distribution of grades. If pupils work hard they will secure higher grades, as there is no artificial ceiling or pre-determined quota to keep them down. The examination boards would deny there ever was.

In many subjects there was also a change in emphasis. The notion of 'investigation' was introduced into the mathematics syllabus. Pupils were expected to mount an inquiry, not just to apply techniques. Music combined listening, composing and performing, so candidates were encouraged to be active musicians, rather than mere analysts of music. A premium was put on reading, writing and speaking in GCSE English language, and some versions permitted 100 per cent of what was awarded to be based on coursework, a controversial matter in which John Major has now intervened personally, as it is disliked by the Right. My son, who took his GCSE last year, wrote 65 pieces of coursework for English, far more than I wrote for O-level, and he is a much better writer than I was at his age.

A subject such as modern languages illustrates the changes. In the O-level, candidates had to translate from English to French and vice versa, write an essay and take a brief oral test. The result was that, after 1,000 lessons in the preceding five years, pupils were nifty at translation, but usually paralysed when confronted with a French customs officer or a German youth hostel warden.

Today's GCSE in languages emphasises oral and written communication about travel, family life, careers, recreation and a series of other everyday topics. Candidates are tested in speaking/listening, understanding, reading and writing at either a basic or higher level, making up to eight tests for the most able. The outcome is that many pupils are able to communicate more effectively than their predecessors, but are less skilled at translation.

I have taught languages for both O-level and GCSE and, though I have some anxiety about the exam and would like to see changes, I have no doubt the shift towards greater emphasis on communication was right. The average pupil nowadays obtains about a grade D, and lest anyone should sneer, I can only say I wish I were at grade D level of competence in Chinese, Japanese, Arabic, Swahili and Greek, as I could more than survive in the various countries.

Veteran teachers report that pupils are working hard for their GCSEs something on which parents have remarked too. More pupils are staying on after the age of 16, and feel successful, although this was bruised by John Patten's ham-fisted handling of the HMI report in September, a few days after one of his ministerial colleagues had congratulated pupils.

Only a careful study, involving multiple re-marking of several years of papers from different boards by experienced markers not knowing from which year or which board the papers came, could tell us whether standards are rising or falling. But the exam boards are unnecessarily defensive about opening up to external scrutiny. Like all exams, the GCSE needs to be changed from time to time. It is a pity the issue has become so political.

Observer, 18.10.92

The fire is out but who will clear up the mess?

Many years ago, two great men held a conversation. One, Winston Churchill, was Prime Minister, the other, R.A. Butler, was the Minister responsible for education. What could be done, Churchill wondered, to make children more patriotic. 'Tell them Wolfe won Quebec,' he mused. In his autobiography, *The Art of the Possible,* Butler related his reply: 'I said I would like to influence what was taught in schools but this was always frowned upon.' 'Of course,' Churchill rejoined, 'not by instruction or order but by suggestion.'

If the wisdom of this conversation had been applied in 1988, there would have been no need for Sir Ron Dearing's announcement last week simplifying the Government's grotesquely complex National Curriculum and testing programme.

Butler's view that politicians should not dabble in the school curriculum was shared by Labour and Conservative Ministers until the arrival of the ambitious Kenneth Baker in 1986. If the Dearing committee was the fire brigade, then it was Baker who had set the chip pan alight.

In his memoirs, Baker will tell of a different conversation between a Prime Minister and an Education Minister, before the 1988 Education Act that introduced the National Curriculum. Margaret Thatcher, he will say, wanted a back-of-an-envelope job with a few basics and not much else. Baker will contend that he then rode up on his white charger and rescued the curriculum from this philistine conception.

This interesting version of history plays down the fact that it was Baker who set up a 10-subject curriculum by establishing 10 different working groups. It was a recipe for disaster. Lock separate groups of subject enthusiasts away in 10 different rooms for a few weeks and they all return wanting half the week for their own discipline.

Baker's ambition to make his mark and underline his position as a future Prime Minister was compounded by his deep distrust of teachers. Part of the necessary macho image for would-be premiers is to appease the right wing of the Conservative Party by being tough on teachers, who are thought by the more fevered to be wild trendies in need of the lash. In order to bring teachers to heel, the National Curriculum was spelt out in minute detail in dozens of folders, booklets and pamphlets.

In 1980 I wrote an article entitled 'Ten steps down the slippery slope to state-approved knowledge'. At that time we had the first step, the Government's stating of general intentions, such as the need to have a broad and balanced curriculum, sentiments at which only psychopaths would have demurred. Now all 10 are in place, as the Government controls the detail of what is taught, how it is tested and what happens to the test scores, and even begins to attack teaching methods and prescribe the books children should read. It is vastly different from the way in which Butler and Churchill operated.

Most other countries have a National Curriculum which is set out in a single slim pamphlet. When I recently opened a fourth and fifth shelf in my study to accommodate the mass of documents produced by our Government on curriculum and testing, I was tempted to invite Kenneth Baker along to do the ceremonial unveiling.

The reason the Dearing committee proposed drastic simplification is clear if you perform the relevant multiplication sum. Teachers have to assess 30 children on 10 subjects at three or more levels. In the original version of the National Curriculum, each subject contained up to 17 different topics or 'attainment targets' and there were two, three or four different statements for each of these at each level.

The original attainment target 11 in science, for example, covered both electricity and magnetism, so each had to be assessed. Multiply up these various elements, and teachers would have to fill in 10,000 to 20,000 different little boxes for one class. If that is education then Kenneth Baker is a banana, as the editor of *Private Eye* might have remarked.

The Dearing committee has made a good start but we need to remember that there are still many problems to be resolved. Five-year-olds have to cover 10 academic subjects, the nine of the National Curriculum plus religious education. This is nonsense.

There should be a massive drive on literacy and there is no point in saddling young children with such a load when they cannot even read. Five domains would be plenty at this stage — literacy at the centre, a numeracy, the world around us (knowledge of your own back-yard, what the Germans call *Heimatkunde*), how things work (elementary science and technology) and the arts (including movement).

Schools can still barely offer choice, such a second language, economics, Latin, health education. If even a slimmed-down curriculum requires most of the week, little will have been gained. Fifty to 70 per cent should be the maximum prescribed.

Furthermore some subjects, particularly technology, revision of which has been deferred, are a conceptual mess, and asking 10 groups to reconvene will not necessarily produce a coherent curriculum.

So thanks for putting out the fire, Ron, but I hope someone is coming in to rebuild the kitchen.

Observer 8.8.93

WHO SAYS TEACHING IS TOO BUSY NOWADAYS?

Chapter 3

Life in the Classroom

Class Conscious?

Have you ever wondered what kind of teacher you are, where you fit into the great scheme of things, whether you should be labelled a traditionalist or a progressive? Following the most rigorous scientific testing, (well, the occasional pilot, all right then, I made it up off the top of my head), I offer this authoritative new test of teaching style, the Bureaucratic and Institutional Grading System for Advanced Teaching, or BIG-SAT, the SAT for really big people. Answer truthfully, unless you are in the running for some kind of bonus payment from your governors, in which case lie like hell.

1. In the first lesson of the year a pupil asks you how you like work to be set out. Do you answer:

(a) I want you to put the date in the left-hand top corner, the title in the middle, and the time to the nearest second in the top right corner. Then underline everything twice neatly with a ruler, the two underlinings being exactly one twelfth of an inch apart.

(b) Search me sunshine. Put what you like as long as I can read it.

(c) Can't you see I'm busy, you little nerd?

2. You see two seven-year-old pupils misbehaving in the far corner of the room. Do you:

(a) Shout, 'Right, that's it. I want you both to stay in at playtime and copy out three pages of Milton's *Paradise Lost.*'

(b) Say, 'That's very nice, children. Now would you like to write a poem about it?'

(c) Carry on swigging from the secret hip flask concealed in your hollowed-out dummy mark book.

3. What is your attitude to children being allowed to move around the room or go to the school library?

(a) Only with my permission, which I never give. My rule about going to the toilet is 'Not until you've turned puce.'

(b) Most of my pupils have usually disappeared to the library or somewhere else anyway.

(c) Library? Classroom? Who cares?

4. A newly appointed head asks you how you deal with spelling. Do you reply:

(a) We have a spelling test every Monday — and every Tuesday, Wednesday, Thursday and Friday, come to think of it. Anyone who makes a mistake has to write it out 10 times in blood.

(b) We did once have a spelling test, but I lost the scoring key, so it never got marked.

(c) Do you happen to have any aspirin with you? Only I've got this thumping head.

5. At an open day for potential applicants to the school, a parent asks you whether you teach tables. Do you respond:

(a) We go up to 100 times 100. I'm doing the 59 times table this week.

(b) We might actually *make* a table, but only if the suggestion comes from the child.

(c) Just remind me again. Are five nines 45, or is it six nines?

6. If asked to describe the walls of your classroom, would you say:

(a) They are in a plain grey colour, so as not to distract the children from their work. The main feature is a chart listing all the kings and queens of England from William the Conqueror to the present day.

(b) There are so many paintings on them that the blu-tac has pulled one of the walls down

(c) Walls? Well a wall is a wall, isn't it? What more is there to say, or have I missed something?

7. How is your classroom laid out?

(a)   The children sit in rows and everyone must face the front so that they can all see clearly what they are copying from the blackboard.

(b)   There are several tables and children either sit at one, lie on the floor, or swing from a light.

(c)   The classroom is fine. I am usually the one who is laid out.

8. Do you call your dog:

(a)   Elbow patch

(b)   A S Neill

(c)   Spot

9. What is your attitude to parents?

(a)   There should be a white line painted in every school playground beside a notice saying, 'Parents and other trespassers proceeding beyond this line will be prosecuted'.

(b)   I revere them for having nurtured the delicate flower that is the child.

(c)   Well , I suppose I ought to be grateful to them since they have provided work for a twentieth of a teacher, or, in this authority, for a thirtieth of a teacher.

10. What would you like to see engraved on your tombstone?

(a)   Had good traditional values

(b)   Far out, man

(c)   Do you happen to have any asprin with you? Only I've got this thumping head.

Your score

If you ticked mainly (a) answers, then you are an arch traditionalist. Ask the governors for a new tweed suit and a pair of sensible black shoes.

If you ticked mainly (b) answers, then you are a raving progressive. Ask the governors for a new string of beads and a trendy suede headband.

If you ticked mainly (c) answers, then you are utterly knackered. Ask the governors for a decent burial.

A forthcoming article by two researchers who gave BIGSAT to a stratified random sample of 1,000 teachers broken down by age and sex (mainly the former, as few could remember the latter) will reveal that 25 were traditional, 25 were progressive, and 950 were utterly knackered. See Splutzenheimer, A. and Goebbels, B. 'The correlation between paracetamol consumption and national testing', in the *International Journal of the Unutterably Futile*, volume 36, number 3, autumn 1991 (in press).

Times Educational Supplement 13.9.91

Headless chickens fricasseed

There is a farm in a part of the country where the RAF practises its low runs, which has a particular problem. Every time a jet comes screaming overhead on an imaginary raid, the hens all rush into the henhouse in such a panic they become wedged and have to be prised back out again. As a response to pressure it reminds me of one of the means that most of us working in education occasionally adopt to cope with stress. Running round like headless chickens before huddling together , more in despair than hope, is a coping strategy that helps us face adversity. There are several others.

Indeed the animal behaviour literature is rich with examples of response to stress that those working in the education service will recognise. In the 1960s the ratologists used to investigate what happened to rats when they had to run across an electrified metal grid to reach their food. The average rat coped with mild shocks, but gave up when things got too painful. Sensitive rats given shocks retired with a nervous breakdown. Loony or delinquent rats hurled themselves defiantly across, even when wired up to the whole national grid. For 'rats' read 'teachers', and for 'national grid' real 'national curriculum', and you will see the parallel. If you have survived, it is probably because you are a loony delinquent.

All the classic defence mechanisms can be witnessed every day in education in textbook form. Consider just a few of them: repression, whereby the unpleasant is pushed out of consciousness altogether ('Kenneth Who?'); reaction formation, in which you display the exact opposite to what you really feel, like excessive politeness towards someone you cannot stand; denial, which involves pretending the problem does not exist ('National curriculum, squire? We've been doing it for years')' and displaced aggression, when anger is diverted to someone other than the real subject, such as kicking the dog because Kenneth Clarke is not personally available.

One aspect of all this which has been a real help in education is that being stressed is now the norm. If every day is fraught, then one more bog-up is neither here nor there, whereas if you only had one crisis a week, then you would probably go into catatonic shock if someone offered you a second biscuit with you cocoa.

Incidentally, you can learn a lot about people during the biscuit ritual. Watch carefully when the biscuits are passed round. I notice, whenever I go to a meeting of our local education committee that the Conservatives grab all the best biscuits, the chocolate ones and those wrapped in gold foil, Labour councillors take the plain ones, and the Lib Dems cannot decide which biscuit to have. As the university member I fill my pockets to take back to students with overdrafts; the teacher members are just grateful for anything that is free, and the officers have to wait until the political members vote in favour of their being allowed to have a biscuit at all, depending on what they decided in their caucus meeting that morning. But back to coping with stress.

A few weeks ago there was forewarning of more stress to come when it was announced that, as several hundred teaching jobs might soon be disappearing under LMS, there would have to be courses for school governors on how to sack people. What on earth would such courses consist of? Is there some accumulated expertise here that has passed the rest of us by? Are there refined techniques well documented in classic texts? Perhaps there lies somewhere in this literature a Baker ('How are you my old friend? How nice to see you, and what a splendid job you're doing. By the way, if you look in the cloakroom you'll find that I've pinned your cards to your raincoat sleeve'), or a Clarke ('Shove off, scumbag, you're fired').

Whenever adversity beckons there are those who will profit from it. When I was a student delivering the Christmas mail, I remember feeling very sorry for an old couple in their eighties who looked out hopefully each day for Christmas cards that never came. Eventually, to their great joy, they got one. It was from the local undertaker.

Many teachers scored high on the stress tests which were popular in Sunday supplements a few months ago — the sort where you add up points for various stress factors, like receiving a parcel from the National Curriculum Council (10 points), discovering the horse you have put the rest of your LMS money on fell at the second fence (50 points), or being trapped in a lift with Kenneth Clarke (250 points). Being willing to support rather than undermine each other, recognising that there is only so much you can do in the time available, and sharing a ghoulish sense of humour in the staffroom, have done much to help teachers survive.

There is an argument, of course, that stress is actually good for you, that it stiffens the coping muscles, so to speak, and makes you a better person. A few years ago one of the great chief education officers of those days was told by the senior adviser that a certain school in the authority was completely underfunctioning. The best solution, in the circumstances, it was decided, was for the CEO to send for the head, who was not doing a hand's turn of work, and really give him hell.

The appointed day came and the poor hapless head was duly wheeled in front of the famous CEO and given such a pasting that County Hall corridors were ringing with the Big Chief's wrath. Eventually the man staggered out looking bemused and shell-shocked. Seconds later the senior advisor rushed, ashen faced, into the CEO's office. 'There's been a terrible error, Sir. You sent for the wrong man. I told you it was Scroggins of Lower Piddlington School who was under-performing , and you've just given a rocket to Boggins of Upper Piddlington School by mistake. No wonder he looked so shattered'. The great man thought for a moment 'Never mind', he said drawing philosophically on his pipe, 'It'll do the bugger good'.

Times Educational Supplement 6.3.92

And for our top scorers, a gilt-edged P45

It is one of the paradoxes of education today that we are about to see teachers being made redundant when we are short of teachers. Here we have the ridiculous situation of schools crying out for staff, while at the same time being compelled to lose teachers, not because they are incompetent, but because the school faces financial difficulties under local management. The very system that was supposed to liberate schools is now shackling them. If you hear a faint scraping noise in the distance, it is probably a visiting Martian scratching his green oblong head with disbelief at the folly of it all.

He would not be consoled, either, by some of the measures being taken to deal with the problem. Alongside courses for governors on how to sack teachers, we now have one local authority drawing up a redundancy points system: the more points you are awarded, the more likely you are to be fired. Apparently teachers are to be awarded points according to length of service, sickness record, contribution to the life of the school, salary and disciplinary record, up to a maximum of 100. If redundancies became necessary those with the most points would be dismissed.

There is something awful about deciding the fate of experienced professional people by formulae. Teaching is not a mechanical act and should not, therefore, be judged by mechanical means. Assigning points to people in this way would bring out the very worst in everyone, the judged and the judges. The idea should be strangled at birth.

It would be much better to turn the whole thing into a popular family board game, where it belongs, and I am tempted to launch it now in time for the usual Christmas bonanza. Purchasers of my new blockbuster *Redundo* will receive a colourful snakes-and-ladders type board, two dice, for it is essentially a game of luck, rotten luck in this case, and the instructions. I originally thought of having the instructions produced by the National Curriculum Council, but nobody would have read them, or alternatively by the School Examinations and Assessment Council, but nobody would have understood them.

The rules are very simple. Participants have their own plastic piece to move round the board, icons of Kenneth Baker, Big Mike Fallon and other well known redundant figures. After throwing the dice, players move their piece the requisite number of places and may land on a square which requires them to take a card from one of the piles. There are three categories of card offering varying degrees of good and bad fortune. Every point you add moves you on a square towards the top of the board and dismissal, whereas each point you subtract moves you back a square towards safety.

The 'tough toe-nails' pack contains statements such as 'you have to stay at home yet again for the carpet-fitter, add 10 points' or 'your N-registered Hillman Imp fails to start and you are late for school, add five points'. The 'jammy beggar' pack offers cards like 'most of your pupils can afford to pay for private coaching and do well on the SATs, subtract 10 points' and 'you qualify for a free course on how to smarm round the governors, subtract 20 points'.

The third pack is entitled 'pot luck' and contains a mixed fortune. You might draw 'you volunteer to take a pay cut, subtract 50 points' or 'you qualify for an additional merit bonus on your salary, add 99 points'. It's a tough game *Redundo*, full of paradoxes, mirroring education today exactly. Just when you think you've done well under one set of conventions, such as increasing your salary, you can find you've stacked up the redundancy points under another, by becoming too expensive to employ.

The Government is very keen on my new game so I'm hoping they will give me an enterprise grant to develop it. They particularly like the competitive element. As in Ludo it is possible to 'knock off' your opponents. When you land on one of the five squares marked 'smartass' you are allowed to nominate an opponent and describe a strategy for out-smarting him. If the referee deems it to be a 'clever' strategy then the opponent is given 20 additional penalty points, but if it is a 'master stroke' then the referee calls out 'Redundo!' and the opponent is sent up to square 100 and dismissed.

A strategy regarded as 'clever' would be to alter someone's mark book so that it looked as if all their pupils had done really badly, or to pay a class to fool about during an inspection. A 'master stroke', on the other hand, would be awarded if you slipped a laxative into a rival's cocoa a couple of hours before an appraisal interview.

The main object of the game is to make sure all the other participants reach square 100 before you do. Once a player arrives at square 100, all the others stand up, point to him, shout 'Redundo!' and present him with a copy of the current issue of *The Times Educational Supplement* with all the jobs in his field marked in highlighter pen. He then has to make a mealy-mouthed speech thanking the governors for all they have done for him and is presented with a framed photograph of Kenneth Clarke. The winners are the last two players left in the game. One becomes head, the other chairman of governors. It is a very cushy assignment as all the pupils have now left for other schools. But this is fair enough since *Redundo* is, after all, a game of chance.

I have given our Martian friend a free sample of the game, but he tells me that he and his friends, despite their immense oblong brains and IQ, of over 2,000, will never be able to work out the rationale behind it. That's because, in the topsy-turvy world that education has now become, there isn't one.

Times Educational Supplement 1.5.92

The tell-tale traits of a
primary staffer

It is easy to spot a member of the armed forces in civvies. Soldiers have short-back-and-sides haircuts, their officers go round with ramrod straight backs revealing their 'military bearing', sailors have a rolling gait and members of the Air Force use words like 'prang'. That at any rate is the conventional stereotype. But how do you recognise primary teachers in mufti?

Some things are missing. For example, there is no Freemason's handshake. If you shake hands with a reception class teacher and find her digits are screwed up at funny angles, it is not because she belongs to a secret society. She has probably just been tying 27 sets of shoe laces and anorak cords. Nor is there a uniform. Most men teachers shed their working jackets with faded leather cuffs and elbow patches at weekends, in favour of something more trendy, like Hush Puppies and flares.

The real giveaways are in movement, gesture and quaint habitual behaviour. I have learned all this through years of detailed observation. If you see someone clutching a clipboard and pen in shopping centres, it is me. I engage people in conversations like, 'You must be a Year 2 teacher in a primary school and you've just been marking children's test papers. Am I correct?' 'That's absolutely amazing, how on earth did you know that?' 'You've forgotten to put any clothes on.'

We stereotypers travel the country compiling our detailed observation dossiers. I offer our findings free, even though commercial operators are willing to pay a fortune for our lists of behavioural traits. This is because they are anxious to track down as many teachers as possible, so they can persuade them to part with their half a per cent salary increase windfall, dangling such goodies before them as second-hand 1974 Hillman Imps, real plastic imitation leather elbow patches, invitations to Oxfam's 'Sale of sales', and re-usable paper handkerchiefs.

Recognising teachers in September is particularly untaxing. At this time teachers have to get to grips with their new class and lay down patterns of acceptable behaviour for the whole year. Look out, therefore, for people in supermarkets whose eyes are out on stalks, rotating frantically in all directions, giving the hunted look of a fugitive master spy.

Those shoppers who buy 27 packets of cornflakes and 27 cylindrical containers of sink scourer, then empty the contents on the pavement outside and take home the empty containers, are not escaped lunatics, but rather reception class teachers preparing for Monday's design and technology session. It used to be called 'junk modelling' until the work 'junk' became reserved exclusively for School Examinations and Assessment Council documents.

Reception class teachers are also recognisable whenever children cry. They are the ones who, at the sound of a five-year-old sobbing, drop all their shopping in the middle of the mall, rush over to the nearest five year-old-boy, grab him by the throat and shout, *'Did you just hit her, Darren Rowbottom?'*.

Year 2 teachers can easily be identified by what we stereotypers call 'assessment drive', the need to assess everything at all times. At the check-out, when the assistant says, 'Three bars of chocolate at 28 pence each, that's £8.79', most people simply protest. The Year 2 teacher, however, replies: 'I'm sorry, you've failed level 2, so lets drop back a level. If I give you five of these blue counters, how many more will you need to make ten?'

Key stage 2 teachers are best recognised by what they say under their breath. The national curriculum is so crammed with factual knowledge that they wander through town muttering to themselves the dates of all the Aztec kings from Montezuma the First, or chanting the atomic numbers in the periodic table of elements from hydrogen to unnilseptium.

The essential *How to Recognise a Primary Teacher* kit is quite easily assembled. It is principally to do with voice and the uncontrollable desire to organise others, plus the feeling that the person concerned is personally responsible if anything goes wrong. Test number one is the voice test. Part A is simple, you merely ask the suspected teacher to read out a sentence. If it can be heard clearly in Oslo, then you can try Part B. This involves speaking the name 'Darren Rowbottom' with six different meanings — threat, enquiry, shock, deep hurt, pleasure and complete contempt. Only teachers can do this. Shakespearean actors come a poor second.

The second test is the organisation test. Find 30 people and ask the suspected teacher to join them. If, 10 seconds later, they are all lined up in twos, preferably holding hands, are marching purposefully to a destination about which they have not been consulted, and no one is running or doing anything silly, then your suspect is probably a primary teacher. If they are also practising their rendering of 'All Things Bright and Beautiful' in very loud but tuneful voices, it is almost certainly a deputy head.

Headteachers are the easiest of all to spot. They are the ones picking up litter. They also argue with shop assistants that the price is high and they want to put it out to competitive tender. When a long queue at the check-out starts getting restless, you can recognise heads with unerring precision. They leap up, should at everyone to stand still, harangue all the old age pensioners, saying, 'You're the oldest, so we expect you to set a good example to others', and finally tell everyone the story of Robert the Bruce and how the spider tried patiently over and over again. Then they leave the shop saying it's all John Patten's fault and go off to organise a boycott.

Times Educational Supplement 19.3.93

The Plowden Retort

What an irony it is that Kenneth Clarke's criticisms of primary education and his setting up of a committee of inquiry should coincide with the 25th anniversary of the much maligned Plowden Report. It was actually in 1963 that another Conservative minister, of a completely different vintage, Sir Edward Boyle, originally asked the Central Advisory Council for Education 'to consider primary education in all its aspects'.

There was nothing punitive about this action, for if the 1980s was the decade of government imposed legislation, the 1960s was one of momentous official committee tomes on every aspect of education.

Three years later, in October 1966, Lady Plowden delivered her committee's two-volume report to a Labour education minister, Anthony Crosland, who described its recommendations as being 'of far-reaching significance'. Little did he realise, when the report was eventually published in 1967, that it would be seen as controversial on its 25th anniversary and would spark off another inquiry lasting weeks not years.

I remember well the publication of the Plowden Report, as I had just started my first job in a university. I read avidly the whole 1,000-plus pages. It was a remarkable account, nothing like it is currently portrayed by politicians, some of whom have probably never read a word of it.

For a start there was a whole chapter on parents, who rarely got a mention in official reports at that time. This bore the hallmark of Michael Young, founder of the Consumer Association. The recommendations included regular parents' meetings, written reports once a year, open enrolment, full use of schools by the community out of hours and parents to assist in school whenever possible. Most of these have become policy today, hardly wild revolutionary stuff.

Indeed, a shrewd government would trace its own 1980s legislation in favour of parents back to the seminal research undertaken for the Plowden Report into the influence of background on children's achievement. A survey of 3,000 children in 173 primary schools showed that parents' attitudes correlated more highly with achievement (on a reading comprehension test) than either home circumstances or the state of the school. This 'mum and dad count most' conclusion offered justification for the spread of parent-teacher associations in the 1970s and legislation in the 1980s.

Other chapters are equally striking. The one on the growth and development of children is superbly written and was, at the time, state of the art, through it looks a little dated now, partly because of the overly deferential treatment of Jean Piaget's stage theory, which led to the conclusion I have always regarded as bunk: 'Until a child is ready to take a particular step forward, it is a waste of time to try to teach him to take it.'

I can remember feeling at the time that this notion could so easily be misapplied as a limiting and conservative influence. For fear of moving too fast teachers might progress too slowly.

The Plowden Report also contains some excellent sections on nursery education (whatever happened to that?), primary/secondary transfer, what at the time were called 'handicapped children in ordinary schools', education in rural areas, teacher training, gifted children, children of immigrants, staff deployment, governors and school buildings. There was a determined attempt to establish real priority areas, so that children suffering social deprivation could learn in schools that had been given a boost in resources. This point was pursued eagerly in the following years, when people such as Eric Midwinter ran imaginative schemes in Liverpool and other cities.

Again the policy recommendation was based on sound research. The committee had commissioned a survey of 83 county boroughs which showed that more money was often spent in areas with the fewest social needs, to the neglect of those in desperate straits. Other research revealed that rickets had begun to recur in some children, that overcrowding was a serious problem in some areas, that poorer people often worked longer hours, and that many homes had not a single book for children. Such findings were grounds for a crusade.

Even in its section on curriculum, the Plowden Report is not always what people claim it to be. On the teaching of reading, for example, it says: 'Children are helped to read by memorising the look of words and phrases, often with the help of pictures, by guessing from a context which is likely to bring them success, and by phonics.' Kenneth Clarke at his most petulant could hardly describe that sober conclusion as barmy, since it is close enough to the advocacy of mixed methods in last year's HMI report on the teaching of reading.

Much of it reads like the national curriculum. In the science section there is criticism of over-reliance on nature study and the lack of work in the physical sciences and scientific processes. Learning by discovery is given some emphasis, but the report cautions against letting children flounder through lack of structure. Words like 'precision' and 'reliability' are prominent and in the English section there is a recommendation that errors should be corrected, especially 'in sentence construction, in punctuation and in spelling which get in the way of communication'.

With so much that is sober-sided, why has the Plowden Report acquired the reputation among right-wing commentators of having undermined standards? It may begin with the statement in the first line of chapter two: 'At the heart of the educational process lies the child', the shibboleth of what is sometimes called 'child-centred education'. But what *should* lie at the centre? The dinner register? As a parent I hope my children are at or near the centre, rather than at the periphery.

Perhaps it is the very existence of choice for children which offends right-wing sensibilities but then the Government itself is strongly wedded to choice for the consumer, and a good educational system should prepare people for the realities of adult life. Choice is something you need to learn to exercise sensibly, not something you are given along with a set of car keys on your 18th birthday.

More likely the Plowden Report is a handy scapegoat, for those who have not read it carefully, for all our real and imagined ills. Taken to extreme, of course, some of its recommendations would be silly, but a subsequent HMI survey concluded that only one teacher in 20 in the 1970s was a way-out progressive. It never advocated that everything should be project work, indiscipline, sloppy standards or daft methods of teaching, so no one should pretend that it did. It summarised what it saw as the best of primary practice, rather than compelled a revolution.

My major criticism would be of its emphasis on 'readiness', when skilful teaching is sometimes about *not* waiting, but finding a neat way of helping children to learn whether they seem ready or not. That aside, I would strongly urge not only critics to celebrate the silver anniversary of the Plowden Report next month by reading or re-reading what is one of the most thorough and imaginative of all government reports, but also Plowden fans, just in case they have forgotten or misapplied what the report actually said.

Times Educational Supplement 12.12.91

Light shed on leading questions

'Are you a packed lunch?' This was one of over 1,000 questions asked by teachers which we have analysed as part of the Leverhulme Primary Project at Exeter University. It is the sort of question that might cause great distress to a Martian, or even confuse an intelligent adult not used to the ways of school, but it posed no problems to a British six-year-old at noon one Monday.

Primary teachers ask numerous questions in a day and they are of several kinds. Most of the ones to do with the substance of the lesson, rather than the management of it, involve the recall of simple factual information, often in small bite-size chunks: How many legs does an insect have? Is a spider an insect? Such questions are often labelled 'closed', with a single answer, verifiable in a textbook. Others are open with several possible answers: Who can tell me something about insects? Some are slightly open, but focused, such as: What sort of things does an insect have on its head?

During explanations of key concepts, teachers sometimes ask a whole string of related questions, in an attempt to probe the idea more thoroughly: 'What are these for?' 'They're feelers,' 'Yes, but what are they for?' 'Feeling things.' 'Yes, but what exactly do they do?'

Some studies have distinguished between higher and lower order questions, arguing that the simple recall of information is at a lower level that, say, analysis, making a generalisation, or using the imagination. This is partly true. Children are clearly operating at a higher level of reasoning if answering a question such as 'What is the difference between a bird and an insect?' than when they merely say how many legs one of them has. On the other hand, 'What is the formula of DNA?' would be a data recall question, but the answer could hardly be called 'lower order'.

One of the surprises we found when analysing teachers' questions during the project was the large number that were about the management and procedures of the lesson. In many lessons, over half the questions asked were about class management, such as 'Oh, Peter, what haven't you done?', a question with a mind-blowing potential infinity of answers ('Repaired the hole in the ozone layer', 'Robbed the Bank of England', 'Built a bridge across the Pacific') until you realise the reply was simply 'writing', as Peter had missed out the caption he had been told to include under his picture.

Many managerial questions are either commands disguised as questions, like 'Would you like to get your books out?' (Try replying, 'Not really, I thought I'd read my comic for a few more minutes' and see what happens), or rhetorical questions where no answer is expected, such as, 'Merilyn, can you sit properly?', which presumably was not inviting a detailed anatomical response and certainly did not get one.

There is no research evidence that one kind of question is invariably superior to another. We may have our individual preferences, but it is not possible to say that a question like. 'What do you think you'd have to take into an air raid shelter?', asked by a teacher whose class was looking at the Second World War, is 'better' than one asking for the dates of the same war. They are simply different. Effective questioning depends on the context: whether the question was appropriate to the child concerned and to the topic being studied, whether the child understood it and replied appropriately, whether it helped or hindered understanding.

Research on questioning can be valuable in that it helps you focus on your own questioning, a skill that lies right at the heart of the primary teacher's classroom craft, even if it only occupies, typically, less than 10 per cent of what you do in a day.

Is the balance between different types of question, closed and open, managerial, lower or higher-order, a reasonable one? Who gets asked questions? Just those who sit in the middle of the room or raise their hands? What does the teacher do when children cannot answer? Ask someone else? Wait? One American researcher found that teachers often waited less than a second and that extending 'wait time' just a little helped elicit more correct replies.

Questioning your own questioning is one of the most valuable steps you can take to improve your teaching.

The 'correct' answer to the question 'Are you a 'packed lunch?', by the way, as any infant school teacher or six-year-old will tell you, is, of course, 'No, I'm a school dinner'.

Times Educational Supplement 21.2.92

Ain't misbehavin'

It is 8.20 am in the down-town area of a large northern city. As the bleak morning light flickers across the broken slates of the grim terraced houses, the first few pupils and teachers are arriving at school. In the playground lies a dead rat. How had it perished? There is speculation among pupils and staff. Perhaps someone had shot it with an air rifle, or maybe it was just a victim of the grimy environment in which it had spent its brief existence. It lay there, another symbol of decay and neglect in a crumbling inner city.

We observed lessons in a wide range of schools in London, the North-west and the South-west when we studied class management during the Leverhulme Primary Project at Exeter University. Some were in idyllic surroundings, others in tough locations. One pupil proudly told his teacher that his father had been on television. Pleased at this mark of recognition of an otherwise ignored sector of society she asked what programme he had appeared in. The answer was BBC national news. He had been shown throwing slates from the roof of a prison during a jail riot.

Yet even in some of these tough schools there was a general feeling of orderliness. We observed 60 teachers in one study and few lessons were disorderly, with 98 per cent of misbehaviour being coded as 'mild'. Rarely was there the sort of pupil-to-pupil violence or insult to the teacher that would have been registered as 'more serious'. The three main categories of misbehaviour were noisy chatter, movement without permission and illicit use of materials, and in 94 per cent of cases the teacher took some action before naughtiness escalated. On 96 per cent of occasions the teacher's action led to an ending or lessening of misbehaviour.

The most common responses from teachers when children misbehaved were orders to cease, the naming of pupils and reprimands. 'Peter Robinson' can be said in a variety of voices by primary teachers, ranging from gentle curiosity to towering rage. One of the more successful strategies observed was involving pupils in their work again. Some teachers merely told people off, but others walked over and shoehorned them gently or firmly back into whatever they were supposed to be doing.

We saw some interesting differences between lessons given in various contexts. London pupils were more likely to engage in noisy or illicit chatter than other children we observed, but were much less likely to be seen wandering round the room without permission. Teachers in the South-west re-involved pupils in their work after misbehaviour more frequently than others in the sample. The most notable difference among pupils was in the category 'pupil altercates or protests'. Whereas in the South-west children only protested on 2 or 3 per cent of occasions when told off, in London it was 12 per cent. Expect a bit more lip from children in our capital city, seems to be the message.

There were also striking differences between classes of different ages. The most badly behaved pupils were the seven to nine age groups and the best behaved were nine to twelve year olds. Seven to nine year olds engaged in much more noisy chatter, inappropriate movement or use of materials and were more defiant towards the teacher. They were also much less likely to stop misbehaving when told off.

Teachers were also different in their behaviour towards older and younger pupils. The use of touch, for example holding someone by the shoulders while steering them gently back to their seat, was observed in 30 per cent of the teachers' responses to misbehaviour by four to seven-year-olds, but with older children there is much more of a touch taboo, and in the case of nine to twelve-year-olds only 7 per cent of responses involved touch.

During each lesson observation we studied every pupil in the class in turn, noting the extent to which they were engaged in the task and whether they were behaving well or badly. Circumstances and social background are often blamed when pupils misbehave, but it was fascinating to see two teachers, sometimes in adjacent classrooms, one where pupils were involved in their work, the other with much more misbehaviour.

Where classes behaved badly there was often lack of clarity about everyday classroom rules. One teacher told the class that they must put up their hands and not wander round the room, then immediately answered questions from pupils who ignored the request, but later remonstrated with someone else for breaking the rule. The arbitrary and random nature of rules seemed directly related to a low work-rate and high level of misbehaviour, as children tried to tease out the rules by trial and error.

Some of the most effective teachers in tough surroundings worked hard to give their pupils a better self-image. One teacher called the class her 'smarties'. The combination of affection, respect for their 'smartness' and the name of the well-known sweet, was just one of several little touches that created a positive climate.

Many of the teachers who secured good relationships and a high degree of attention to work in hand showed a good sense of humour. 'Jason, it won't help if you are chopping her head off with a ruler,' said one, before defusing a potentially tricky situation with a difficult child. She had inherited a class that was behind with its work, and would occasionally call for a round of applause for someone who had made a special effort. When she asked them to give themselves a pat on the back, many did it literally. As with others we observed, her effectiveness lay partly in her raising the children's self-image by alerting the whole group to positive achievements, clear rules fairly and consistently enforced, all deftly-laced with well-received humour.

Times Educational Supplement 21.5.92

Shout and be damned

'The lady who's in there,' said six-year-old Darren, pointing to the teacher in the next room, 'she kept on shouting at us and we couldn't get on with our work. But I done it good, so I didn't get told off.'

Darren was one of 460 pupils from different parts of the country we interviewed as part of the Leverhulme Primary Project to discover what they think about class management. Children are crystal clear about their taste in these matters, and they definitely do not like teachers who shout all the time.

In fact, if there is one area of educational research where the findings have been astonishingly consistent over the years it is pupils' views of teachers and teaching. In 1935 a questionnaire was given to 8,000 children in Birmingham about effective teaching. Highest ranking was accorded to teachers' ability to explain difficulties patiently.

In 1984 I administered a much more detailed questionnaire with 32 items to a sample of 200 secondary children. Top of their list was the ability to explain clearly. Children also want teachers to be slightly strict, use rewards and punishments fairly, be interested in them as individuals and have a sense of humour, without being sarcastic.

In our interviews we used three large photographs. The first showed two pupils sitting at the same table pushing each other, the second was of a class barging into the room in an unruly manner after playtime, and the third was of a girl, brought out to the front of the class for scribbling on someone's book, who had just called the teacher 'old cow' under her breath. We also asked children what they thought the 'best' and 'worst' teachers in the world would be like, what children do when they're naughty, and how teachers respond.

The response to the photographs were fairly consistent. Children expect that two pupils pushing each other will be told off. They may be sent outside, moved to separate seats or even sent to the head. Rushing into the room after break also earns a telling off, and they will be shouted at, probably sent outside to come in again properly. The girl who has insulted the teacher will get the full works, be told off and sent to the head, but other pupils visible in the photograph will be reprimanded if they are smiling. Threats to the teacher's authority are a serious matter in children's eyes.

Children's responses to the photographs were not always the same as those of their teachers, to whom we showed the same pictures. Teachers tend to give detailed strategic responses about what they would do and why and a telling off is mentioned less frequently. Yet when we observed the same teachers in their own classrooms, orders to cease and reprimands were in fact the most common responses to misbehaviour.

In that respect children's perceptions were closer to the reality of classroom events. In classes where the teacher in real life shouted a great deal, the children's response to pictures was that the teacher would shout, but no teacher replied 'I would turn into a howling dervish'.

When it comes to what is and is not allowed in class the children are very crisp about those classrooms where the teacher had clear and consistent rules.

'We're not allowed to scream, we're not allowed to shout, we're not allowed to throw things around the classrooms, not allowed to be naughty, we're not allowed to do mean things to people, like scratch and punch and kick and that's it really' (seven-year-old).

'If you haven't finished and you've had a long time to do a certain piece of work then you've got to stay in at break and finish it, and if it's like near the end of the day, then you've got to take it home and finish it for homework' (10-year-old).

The best teachers in the world would, according to these children, do interesting activities, know their stuff, be quite strict, have a sense of humour, and would not be bossy, shout all the time, give unfair punishments, or set work that is too hard. It is a view that is extremely close to the timeless stereotype of earlier studies, a combination of being in charge, but also in possession of the craft skills of teaching, seeing children as individuals, understanding their difficulties and then explaining to them clearly. One 11-year-old summed it up through his vision of the world's worst teacher:

'They'd get cross at the slightest thing and they'd go round not really noticing. They'd go round teaching people and they'd get cross if you got things wrong, instead of seeing how you got it wrong and making sure you understand.'

I suspect every teacher in the land will cringe at that description. It sounds like all of us on a bad day. Ah, if only they understood the problem I'm having with all the marking, then there's the deputy head, the forms to fill in, and the mortgage...

Yet consider the poor little beggars trying to make sense of it all. In the words of one not too sanguine eight-year-old, the beckoning world of adult life can weigh heavily:

'We're not allowed to muck about, we're not allowed to fight, and we're not allowed to yell at the top of our voices, and a few other things which I can't remember. We've got quite a lot of rules — loads.'

Times Educational Supplement 29.5.92

The shock of the new

Every September a traditional set of rituals is repeated in thousands of primary schools: five year olds start school for the first time; six-year olds return to find they are no longer the novices of their school; seven-year olds move on to the junior school, or to a higher class in their present school; parents wonder whether their children will settle in; teachers establish relationships with their new class, meet new pupils, renew acquaintance with others they have taught before.

Not surprisingly, these first encounters have been less well documented and analysed than later phases in the year. When researchers seek to visit and observe classes early in the year they are often asked to come back in late September or early October 'when things have settled down'. First encounters can be private affairs, even in schools which are normally open to observation and scrutiny, and teachers realise they are not always themselves during these first few days, eyes out on stalks, leaping around the school, larger than life.

As part of the Leverhulme Primary Project we observed 20 experienced teachers during the first week in September to see how they managed their very first lessons with their new class, and we then saw 16 student teachers during the first few days of their teaching practice. There were some interesting comparisons.

When we interviewed the teachers the previous July, most said they had not met the children they were going to teach, except in the playground. Three quarters, however, mentioned the class's existing reputation, one saying 'Every school has one class no teacher would like to teach. This is one of them'. Many said that they had resolved to be more strict and formal with the class than their predecessor had been, and to demand higher standards of work .

There was a stark contrast between the first days in primary schools and observations I did a few years ago of secondary classes in early September. The secondary teachers tended to be more aggressively assertive, quick to pounce on misbehaviour and occasionally humiliate early miscreants chancing their arm. 'Firm but friendly' would be a better description of their primary teachers' first few lessons. Statements like 'Hands please, let us have manners at all times' and 'For the moment, I'm the boss. No talking when the teacher is talking' were typical of the establishment of ground rules on the first morning .

Early September sees a huge effort made by the whole school to launch the new year. On the first day, teachers are more likely to escort the class into the room and make greater use of commands'Always bring a book to class', 'Bring exact change for dinner money', 'Always underline your work with a ruler, it looks neater' and the bizarre 'Don't eat pencils' were all examples of this greater directiveness.

The first assembly often reinforced this clean new image, and heads exhorted children to use common sense, think about others. follow school rules. Older pupils were frequently reminded publicly that they were now top of the school and should set an example. One head told the story of Robert the Bruce to urge children to try their best at all times. Others stressed orderliness in assembly: 'When you come into assembly, imagine a zip across your mouth. It is your responsibility to keep it closed'.

By contrast, the student teachers, starting their long teaching practice in April, suffered from two disadvantages. First, they were less clear in their own minds what their rules and expectations of children were, and second, the big collective effort made by the whole staff back in September was only a faint memory. On the other hand they did not have the playground duties and other tasks such as setting up classroom routines, that experienced teachers had been obliged to fulfil.

Attention-getting was sometimes a problem, and the unconvincing 'Shhh' often needed a second go, sounding more like a Schweppes advert than a command for silence. The greatest difficulty many faced was individual badly behaved pupils, some of whom, by way of a 'welcome aboard' gesture, put on a special display of their disruptive talents in the very first lesson.

My enduring memory of the research is of a reception class in a school in a very tough area. The last child to be brought in, at about 10.30 on the first morning, screamed at her mother all the way down the corridor and then kicked a supply teacher firmly on the shin when the latter tried to console her. After her mother left, the reception class teacher incorporated her brilliantly, encouraging her to do a jigsaw, make a model and build with some blocks. She was completely absorbed all day.

At 3.30 an ashen-faced mother arrived to collect the child who promptly burst into tears. She must have been convinced that her daughter had been on the rack all day, yet the girl came happily to school for the rest of the year. Meanwhile I made a mental note that any five-year-old whose first reaction to a teacher was to kick her could have a great future as a politician.

Times Educational Supplement 11.9.92

The most delicate balancing act

It is strange how whole-class teaching has become a political issue. The Government appears to want more of it, yet without any evidence that either more or less whole-class teaching would be a good thing.

As part of the Leverhulme Primary Project we observed 60 teachers in primary schools all over the country in both urban and rural areas. One of the techniques we used was to sample lessons at various stages to see what kind of teaching was taking place. As a result we were able to analyse nearly 1,200 'snapshots', that is two-minute lesson segments, during which we documented when the teacher was teaching the whole class, or whether there was individual and group work.

What emerged was that teachers spent roughly one-third of their time on whole-class teaching. Just under two-thirds of lesson time consisted of pupils working alone or in groups, almost always with the teacher monitoring. Only in 2 per cent of lesson segments was the teacher not monitoring. About 4 per cent of lesson segments analysed showed transitions from one activity to another, sometimes with, sometimes without movement. Lest anyone should think that student teachers only use 'trendy' methods, it must be pointed out that a sample of student teachers we studied spent about half their time on whole-class teaching.

When we looked more closely at whole-class teaching it divided almost exactly into another two-thirds/one third split. Within whole-class time about two-thirds was teacher-pupil interaction, and one-third consisted of the teacher addressing the class solo. We also analysed the responses of teachers to misbehaviour. About a quarter of these were to the whole class, the remaining three-quarters was split evenly between individuals and small groups.

The most common reaction I get from lay people, journalists and politicians when I talk about this one-third/two thirds split between whole-class teaching and individual or group work is: 'What *should* it have been?'. The assumption is that there is a single paragon mix, some ideal blend of whole-class and other forms of teaching. It is a quest for fool's gold or the philosopher's stone, for there is no universal perfect mix. Whether a teacher uses whole-class teaching or not depends on the context.

Those who believe that teaching the whole class is always best, should ask themselves whether they would have wanted to learn to drive a car by sitting with a group of 30 fellow learners, and listening to a lecture on the clutch, or the braking system. Presumably they would prefer individual practical work. Equally those who claim that class teaching is never desirable, should ask themselves whether they think that, at story time, teachers should whisper the same story 30 times into 30 left ears, rather then tell it to the whole class.

Whole-class teaching is often called the 'traditional' approach. In Victorian times, with huge classes and very few qualified teachers, there were not many choices available. Nowadays the choice of overall teaching strategy is wider, especially with the development of new technology, such as television, the microcomputer and, before long, the spread of interactive videodisk and 'virtual reality'. Rather than attempt to prescribe some universal approach, it is better to encourage teachers to try a range of options, and to think critically about the context in which they use them.

Times Educational Supplement 19.2.93

A five-day week in the lions' den

'I can't cope with two of them, so I don't know how that woman manages with 30.' The speaker was a mother that I interviewed some years ago. Her children, aged six and eight, led her a merry dance at home and she could not understand how a teacher coped.

The Leverhulme Primary Project, which we conducted at Exeter University, was one of the largest studies of primary teaching ever undertaken in this country. My own part of the investigation was into different aspects of teachers' class management, which is much more complex than is commonly realised. In a busy day teachers have to manage several different tasks, their own and those undertaken by their pupils, as well as pupil behaviour, resources, the use of time and space, the application of rewards and punishments, relationships, tensions, conflicts and their own repertoire of teaching strategies.

Class management is often seen as something unidimensional. In the popular mind it is perceived as 'discipline' and little else. Yet the control of pupils' behaviour and dealing with disruption when it occurs, though time and energy consuming in classrooms where there is severe misbehaviour, is only a small part of management in many classes. Much more energy is spent on classroom routines, resource management, looking after the task in hand, deciding which strategy to use in each situation, or monitoring progress.

In the Leverhulme project we studied teachers at the beginning of the school year, meeting their new classes for the first time, and saw the skill with which first encounters were managed. In most classes, rules became clear quickly and were fairly and consistently enforced. In those classes where this was not the case, relationships soon broke down and behaviour deteriorated, as children 'tested the limits' to see what was and what was not permitted. 'Firm but fair' was how most teachers saw themselves in these first few days.

Our studies of classroom behaviour revealed that most misdemeanours are noisy talk and illicit movement; there was very little of the mayhem portrayed in the popular press. Visiting Martians would describe the average primary class as orderly, but might comment on the amount of chatter not relevant to the task in some classrooms. They would be more likely to hear children being lippy to the teacher in city, rather than country, schools. When pupils were told off, arguments with the teacher occurred in about 12 per cent of classes in London schools, compared with 2 or 3 per cent elsewhere.

We interviewed more than 400 children to see what they thought about pupil behaviour. Most were aware of what would get them into bother. One six-year-old showed a clear understanding of the tolerance for mock fights but not for the real thing. 'I just plays on my own with my cousin and some of my friends. We plays a little fight, it's not a real fight, it's a play fight. You just pretend to punch like that (demonstrates mock blow)... You won't get told off...You stand near the wall when you're naughty. I don't stand near the wall. I don't be naughty outside.' I suppose the National Curriculum Council will now be cross with our researcher for not leaping in and teaching him how to conjugate a verb in the present tense.

In one particularly interesting exercise we showed photographs of disruption to both teachers and pupils. According to pupils, teachers would shout a lot in response, but teachers' own replies were much more guarded, and not one used the word 'shout', though most did yell when exasperated. 'I shout at children' is not a phrase that most of us can get through our lips, and you can probably be locked up for it under the Children Act .

I found our studies of questioning and explaining particularly fascinating. Some questions are incomprehensible out of context: 'Have you hidden your tongues?' (to a class that failed to answer a question). 'Did I say go and do a quick scribble?' (to a child whose work was unsatisfactory). About 57 per cent of questions we analysed were to do with management. Only 8 per cent were the sort of higher-order questions that required more than just the recall of information, and I found this a bit disturbing. Though there is no ideal ratio of one type of question to another, my own objective judgement of both the primary and secondary lessons I have analysed is that there is a place for more questions that invite speculation, analysis, grouping and labelling, or a leap of the imagination.

Explaining is the skill most admired and respected by children, and we looked at successful and unsuccessful explanations of topics like 'insects' and 'electricity'. Effective explanations had clear central ideas expressed in appropriate language, examples were usually elicited from pupils rather than given all the time, and the teacher's voice was clear and well modulated. Some ineffective explanations were factually wrong, as teachers struggled to explain scientific principles they did not fully understand themselves, especially in answer to unexpected questions.

Successful explanations were a pleasure to behold, I saw one teacher in a small market town whose pupils all scored virtually full marks in a test given after his lesson on insects. 'Is a bird an insect?' was his starting point, and he built skilfully on the responses to this opening teaser, a 'not' analogy. When I suggested he should write about his teaching, especially as he had so many good ideas, he was overcome by modesty and the fear that his four colleagues might think he was showing off. Imagine surgeons being bashful about their new techniques.

It is a pity that so much debate about primary teaching is stereotyped around crude opposites, like 'traditional' and 'progressive'. Anyone who looks closely at classrooms, would see that a much more subtle and fine grain analysis is needed.

Times Educational Supplement 28.5.93

The waiting game that brings rich rewards

I often ask student teachers to guess how long teachers spend making a decision in the classroom after pupils have answered a question, or when someone misbehaves. 10 seconds is a common guess. Try counting out ten seconds of silence sometime. In classroom terms, especially during a period of rapid interaction, it is an eternity. Many decisions are made in one second or less.

During the Leverhulme Primary Project I was particularly struck by the speed with which certain events unfold. It is an astonishing feat to put together information about a pupil response or a piece of behaviour, diagnose what needs to be done, given the particular child or group concerned, sum up the previous history of similar events, make a selection of the most desirable strategy in the circumstances and then act, all within a second. It is especially impressive when the decision seems pretty sound as well.

Primary classrooms are full of rapidly changing events. The American researcher Philip Jackson found that teachers engaged in about 1,000 interpersonal transactions in a single day. I have studied teachers who ran at rates as high as 1,400. There is sometimes a change in who speaks and who listens as frequently as every three or four seconds. This means that there is often too little time to reflect deeply during a lesson.

I remember reading Chomsky's arguments about transformational grammar and the nature of language in the 1960s. It struck me at the time that there are considerable similarities between his notions of 'deep' and 'surface' structures and theories about teachers' actions in the classroom. If we make decisions quickly, it is because they are founded on certain deeply embedded principles. That is why student teachers are much more hesitant, as their deeper structures are not yet fully laid down.

Take the case of this teacher we heard explaining about insects to his class of nine-year-olds.

Teacher: A camel is not an insect, why?
Pupil: It hasn't got antennae.
Teacher: A snail has got antennae.
Pupil: Insects have wings.
Teacher: So do nightingales.
Pupil: Insects collect pollen.
Teacher: So do humming birds.

This rapid-fire exchange seems to be based on the deep principle that children should be challenged intellectually. As a result, the teacher's lessons are often lively and children are pressed, benignly, into thinking about what they are learning.

This kind of machine-gun dialogue can often be very effective, but the American researcher Mary Budd Rowe, whose own investigations showed that the average gap between speakers was often a second or less, argued that teachers should also sometimes extend 'wait time', as this can produce more profound answers.

If teachers do have deep and surface structures that affect how they teach, then this underlines the need for active reflection on teaching strategies. It is valuable to spend some staff planning time looking at strategies for asking questions, for example.

At their meeting teachers can take a particular topic and discuss the questions they might ask. If these are then written down and analysed, valuable group discussion can occur which gets into the deeper structures that influence classroom practice. It is time well spent.

Times Educational Supplement 28.5.93

Bugs ironed out of explanations

'And in a packed programme today we'll be meeting a man who can yodel under water, I'll be talking to the woman who earned £10,000 legally in just one day, and later we'll show you how to be a clog-dancing champion. But first, the news headlines.'

That sort of intriguing, attention-grabbing opener to a radio or television programme is known as a 'tease'. It is one of numerous devices used by broadcasters to arouse and then hold your interest. Primary teachers use a similarly wide range of strategies, as we have found during the Leverhulme Primary Project at Exeter University.

Studies of pupils' own views of teaching have consistently shown that the ability to explain something clearly is one of the most prized teaching skills, so we decided to make 'explaining' a specific focus in the project.

We often asked numerous teachers to explain a particular topic to their class. One of the themes we chose was Insects, and we were able to observe and analyse 64 lessons in classes of eight and nine-year-olds. A rich variety of approaches emerged.

Questions are a central part of many explanations, as they enable you both to check what pupils already know as well as develop their thinking further. Some questions were 'closed' with a single verifiable textbook answer, such as 'How many legs does an insect have?' Others were 'open' with several possible answers, some of which might not be so easy to verify, such as 'Who can tell me something about insects?' Most teachers used a mixture of styles, sometimes sequencing different types to probe more deeply.

There was considerable variety and ingenuity in practical work. Children caught insects, looked after them, drew or painted them, made them out of pipe cleaners, studied pictures, models, specimens, with or without magnifying glasses. Most teachers recognised the need for some kind of concrete experience to deepen understanding.

This need for the concrete also came out in the use of examples and analogies. Most teachers gave or sought examples of insects, and some used clever analogies, like the one who said: 'Now an insect's eye is rather special, not like ours. It is made up of hundreds of tiny separate eyes and looks almost like a plastic bag of marbles: the plastic bag is the whole eye and the marbles are the mini eyes or lenses.'

Sometimes use was made of a 'not' analogy. By comparing an insect with a bird, an elephant or something that was not an insect, children learned what the essential characteristics were. The teacher whose children scored most highly in a test of insect identification, actually began his explanation with the question 'Is a bird an insect?'

The most interesting broadcaster's 'tease' I came across was no attention-getting gimmick, for it was rich in information as well as intrigue. The teacher began: 'If I told you in, say, a bucket of earth there were hundreds of them. They're in the air, they're even in ponds and rivers. There are millions of them in a tree. They live all over the world, except at the North and South Poles... What do you think I would be talking about?' They were all bursting to do the topic by the end.

Even in factual explanations there was sometimes a touch of the imagination. 'Do you know that butterflies can taste with their feet?' one teacher said to laughter from the class.

The most important features of effective explanations seem to be clear key concepts with good links between them, choice of the right language (knowing when to say 'inversely proportional', when to rephrase it as, 'The more you have of this, the less you have of that', or make it concrete, like, 'It's like a see-saw, the higher this side is the lower that one is'); checking what children know; adding a touch of relevant humour; and giving or eliciting a crisp summary.

The fascinating feature of something like explaining is that you can always try to get better at it, there is so much to learn. Since most teachers give thousands of explanations every term, and since it is a professional skill so highly rated by pupils, it is worth the effort.

Times Educational Supplement 11.10.91

Chapter 4

Management Blues

Selling Swinesville with porky pies

Ah, come in Brian. I'm sorry to drag you away from school, but we at Ramsbottom's Pork Pies are very busy at the moment, so I'm afraid I couldn't nip out today.

That's all right, Mr Ramsbottom, I'm only missing assembly. But I hope it's nothing serious.

Well it is, Brian, it is. You see, when I became chairman of Swinesville High School governors, I was as you know, determined to put the school on the map. That's why we appointed you as head. I thought with your 20 years in the meat pie business here at Ramsbottom's, and six months as a licensed teacher, you were just the man to get the school the image we need. But I have to say I'm very disappointed in you Brian, very disappointed indeed.

But why, Mr Ramsbottom? I've tried to do all that you and the Government have asked of me. We've got the brand new logo, for example.

It's not the logo, Brian. I like the logo. I must say I would have preferred a whole pork pie, rather than just the half, but I do like it.

But we had to leave a bit of room for the mustard, Mr Ramsbottom, so it fitted in with the new school motto, 'Firm as a good pie, keen as mustard'.

I know, I know, Brian, but it's not the logo I wanted to see you about.

What is it then, Mr Ramsbottom?

It's about all these good school guides that have been appearing. What I want to know is, why aren't we in any of them? I've looked through the lot and we're nowhere. Look, we're not in this one here, 200 Smashing Schools by Felicity Fforbes Ffrench, we're not in the Foxhunters' Weekly supplement 99 Tip Top Private Schools and One Decent

State School. We're not even in the Swinesville Gazette's back page article on Swinesville's 10 Best.

It's very hard to get into these guides, Mr Ramsbottom. Even the top 10 in the Swinesville Gazette isn't easy. Goodness knows I've tried hard enough.

But there are only 11 schools in Swinesville, Brian, I mean, what's happened to all those promises you made at your interview? You said you'd get us into the media but so far you've done nothing. The only time the school has been in print was when we advertised that second-hand boiler in Exchange and Mart.

That's not true. I did get Sharon and Darren Barron on to Blockbusters.

Don't talk to me about Blockbusters, I never thought I'd live down the humiliation when Sharon said: 'Give me an 'S' Bob, and he said, 'What 'S' is a vegetable much beloved of Popeye?' And what did Darren reply? I'll tell you what he said, 'Spuds'. I could have died Brian.

But I've tried everything. When you said we should improve our A-level statistics I only entered the two pupils who passed the mocks, so that got us up to 50 per cent this year. Then I forced everybody to stay on at school instead of leaving, except for Darren who was made school caretaker, so that gave us 100 per cent employment rate. What else could I have done?

Well, I've been looking at these guides, and I think I know where we're going wrong. You see, the first thing I've noticed is that the heads of the schools that get into the guides are always a bit of a character. Look at this one, for example, the head of Upper Piddlington College, 'Rides up and down the corridors on his Harley Davidson'. Then locally there's Miss Ruminant of Swinesville Girls' High, 'County underwater ten pin bowling champion'. Or what about the head of St Swithin's Academy, 'Sets fire to his hair during assembly'? You've got to try harder to be a bit of a nutter, Brian.

I'm the only head in Swinesville who's read all the national curriculum documents. Is that the sort of thing you're looking for?

Well that sounds fairly crackers to me, Brian, see what else you can come up with. But there's another thing about getting into these guides. I've noticed that it's all right to have a crazy head as long as you're traditional. Now it seems to me that what we need is an even older tradition than the others, so why don't we have a school uniform that's a few hundred years old? I've been looking at some history books, and I'm going to ask the governors to require everybody to wear doublet and hose, a ruff and carry a pike.

But what about the children on free school meals? I know you give them all a Ramsbottom mini-Krusty for lunch every day, but how will they afford the uniform?

Now that brings me to another thing, Brian. A lot of these good school guide places are sponsored by industry. We'll be offering a free pike with every Ramsbottom's Jumbo Family-size pork-pie, and a free ruff with each Flaky Puff Pasty, as a special promotion under the slogan 'A pike with your pie, and a ruff with your puff'. And while we're at it, I'd like to do something for the teachers.

Oh, they'd appreciate that Mr Ramsbottom.

You have to do everything you can to get the best staff nowadays, Brian, and I'll be offering free health insurance to all the teachers. But there's a special reason for this. You see, I noticed that the staff of the schools that get into these good school guides are usually described as 'very willing', so I've booked the whole of Swinesville Private Clinic next week. We'll close the school for the week and the staff can have the best medical treatment.

That's a very good idea, Mr Ramsbottom. You mean, get the best doctors on to them so that they come out like athletes?

No, not exactly athletes, Brian,.

Well, if the doctors don't turn them into athletes, what do you want them turning into, Mr Ramsbottom?

Eunuchs, Brian, eunuchs.

Times Educational Supplement 4.10.91

Let's have a big hand for the chief chimp

Question 1: Write a sentence using the words 'perform' and 'performance'.

Well, all right, here goes.

'Trained sea lions and chimps perform in the circus and are therefore paid with performance-related fish or bananas'.

Question 2: 'The chief chimp should be paid with a huge hand of bananas if the other chimps perform well'. Discuss.

Ah, now this one is a bit more tricky, but never mind. 'Chief chimps carry a lot of responsibility — making sure the hoops are OK before the rest of the chimps hurtle through them; seeing there are enough tea bags for the party and sweeping up their colleagues' droppings after the show. So they should be given lots of bananas to recognise this. But the other chimps lead a fairly stressful life nowadays, so they should also receive a decent allocation of fruit'.

('Too wimpish. Needs to be more tough-minded' — Examiner)

Question 3: Comment on the performance indicators which are applied in determining the salaries of chimps and chief chimps.

Good, a nice opportunity to show I know the difference between quantitative and qualitative measures here. 'The problem with traditional performance indicators in the circus is that they concentrate on the easily measurable. Thus chimps are paid one banana for each hoop they jump through. The more successful soon become obese, get wedged in the hoop, then receive no pay at all and eventually starve to death. When chief chimps receive huge hands of bananas simply for their colleagues' rather than their own efforts, it is greatly resented. This is a flinty-hearted market perspective. Attention should be paid to the quality of what chimps do, like how skilfully they show humour during the tea party'.

('As an accountant I cannot agree that this view of life should inform an intelligent performance-related chimp pay scheme'— Examiner).

('As a human being I cannot agree that accountants with your views are an intelligent form of life' — Candidate).

Question 4: How should league tables be used to determine chief chimps' remuneration?

'Preferably not at all. Although some chimpologists believe that chief chimps are highly motivated by league tables, others argue that these can have a bad effect. There was the notorious occasion when the audience laughed because a chimp broke wind noisily during a show. Marvo Baked Beans Corporation Inc immediately sponsored a wind-breaking league and chaos ensued'.

('This is far too negative a view of the use of league tables' — Examiner)

('Well sod off then' — Candidate).

Enough of the chimps. The reality is that, in these market-mad times, a monumentally crass view will soon be taken of the best way of rewarding teachers and heads. The 'children are cans of peas' philosophy decrees that teachers should be paid according to their school's place in the league table. This is bad news for all those who work in down town areas, teach slow learners or face classes with more than their fair share of disruptive pupils. The message from the government is clear: 'If you want a pay rise, sunshine, move to a posher school'. It does wonders for teacher stability and morality.

'Ah', the mad marketers will reply, 'but it is only right that the teachers in the schools with the best exam results should be paid most'. (Actually, the maddest marketeers would do nothing of the sort. They would be more likely to put their index finger in their left ear and say, 'Dooby dooby doo, I'm a petunia', but I digress). According to that particular line of argument teachers should be paid far more than doctors. After all, the people teachers deal with are mainly healthy, whereas those that doctors deal with are usually sick, so they can't be much cop on the health front.

No need to worry, the next stage of the argument goes. There will be several performance indicators, not just one, including such features as league tables of truancy rates. This is an approach which has worked in other fields of employment, and was warmly welcomed by mortuary superintendents and the governor of Sing Sing. It might even be worth your while paying people to play truant at the beginning of the year, so you can demonstrate a dramatic improvement by the end of it.

I wonder what thought has been given to how these truancy league tables will be assembled. The official definition of truancy is 'absence without cause'. Will an enormous squad of education welfare officers be hired to check the status of every single absentee, including those with a mere cold or cough? Is the head supposed to guess whether the absence is with or without cause, and if so, on what grounds? Hearsay? Lack of, or ambiguous absence note? ('I am sorry our Albert was away from school last week, owing to a severe upper respiratory infection and recurring attack of 'Let's-spring-clean-and-then-decorate-the-front-room' disease'). Will parents sue if someone makes the wrong guess and labels their child truant? And in cases of doubt are heads supposed to put someone down as a truant and thereby lower their own salary and place in the league table?

The problem with rewarding 'performance' in this crude manner is that it will invite subversion. There will probably be a miraculous reduction in reported truancy rates when they are league tabled. When America went performance indicator mad and tested everyone in sight, one academic decided to look at every state's test scores to see which were above and which were below the national average. He discovered that every single state had published test scores that were above the national average.

I am not opposed to teachers who work hard and do a good job being paid more, but if a system that rewards merit is going to be introduced, why can it not be done in a properly sensitive and sensible manner? If there is some anxiety about linking appraisal and merit pay, then we can learn from the research done by the General Electric Company in the United States, which suggested separating the appraisal interview in time from merit pay decisions, so the two processes complement but do not confound each other. In the meantime, keep honing your skills. The bananas are in the post.

Times Educational Supplement 15.11.91

Feeling a pang of inspector remorse

One feature of the recent assassination of Her Majesty's Inspectorate bothered me a great deal. It was not so much that, where advice to the Government was concerned, we could now say, 'Goodbye HMI, hello rotating eyeballs faction', though that was bad enough. It just seemed a bit naughty, I thought, to announce that HMI would have to write the *How to Inspect a School*, manual for these new privatised inspection companies.

That was really rubbing their noses in it. It was akin to asking a condemned man to build his own scaffold, or the Royal Family to cook lunch for the paparazzi. Given that one replaces an institution with something better, it does seem barmy that what is looked for in the new inspection companies is such complete ignorance of what is entailed that the previous incumbents have to write the *Beginner's Guide* for the mob that takes over. Presumably the rationale for it is based on Kenneth Clarke's own experience that the principal qualification for any job should be knowing absolutely nothing about it.

The temptation to write a manual that will comprehensively stitch up the incoming privatised inspectors must be overwhelming, but we must be sensible about these things, so I thought I might write my own *Amateur Inspector's 'Andy 'Andbook* for these spanking new naive punters.

First, on the question of recruitment, it must be remembered that Kenneth Clarke said that anyone can inspect a school, so this must be taken literally. Selection panels should discourage candidates who appear to know what happens in a classroom. Applicants with teaching experience are clearly barred. Look for people who say 'Search me squire', when asked about the national curriculum.

The correct answer to 'How should teachers deal with disruptive pupils?' is 'Give 'em a kick up the backside, if you ask me'. Select an estate agent to write the report and a bus or taxi driver to take the privatised team to the next school, preferably one who starts the interview with, 'Teachers guv? I'd string 'em all up. 'Ere, I once 'ad that fat git Kenneth Clarke in the back of my car.'

The next section is on what to do at the start of your visit to a school. Here it is important to remember to ask secondary teachers questions like, 'How many children are taking their matriculation?' or to say, 'Gosh, they sit round tables nowadays, do they?' when inspecting a primary school. Establish rapport by telling teachers that you envy them their job and wish you could knock off at three o'clock every day. As they have usually never heard this little joke before, they will laugh merrily and warm to you. It will appeal especially to Year 2 and GCSE teachers.

Once you have endeared yourself to the staff in this way, have a friendly chat with the headteacher. A jolly little jape which goes down well with female heads, by the way, is to ask them if they can direct you to the headmaster. When they explain that they are in charge, ask them if they feel it is really a man's job and shouldn't they be at home making the tea. This will have them in stitches, so you will be on firm ground from here on in. Male heads like to be asked why they didn't take a proper job in industry. They also respect insights like, 'Those who can, do. Those who can't teach'.

There are a few fuddy HMI traditions which are not really worth keeping. One is that inspectors do not go on hearsay, but only report what they have observed themselves. This is clearly a silly thing to do, because most really interesting scandal is based on gossip and rumour, so this should be an essential part of your report. In primary school inspections point out that children seem to play all day and that none of them can read. Secondary school pupils are usually high on drugs most of the time, or at least drunk outside the school gates. The Co-op check-out and the saloon bar of the *Dog and Partridge* are fruitful places for this sort of valuable information.

Inside the school, the most useful gambit for the amateur inspector is what we call the 'Mirror Technique'. What you do here is ask various people what is wrong with the school. You then feed this back absolutely straight and unadulterated. You need to announce it, however, in an assured *ex cathedra* voice, so that it has conviction. People like to hear their own words spoken by someone else, and it does not matter that you may not understand what you are saying, so long as you sound authoritative.

When it comes to the actual report your taxi driver and estate agent will come in particularly useful, depending on what the chairman of governors wants of you. If you are being paid for a whitewash job, then the estate agent is your man. Leaking roofs, peeling paint and water running down walls will become 'an original and untouched highly desirable olde worlde environment'. Lack of books and equipment will turn into 'traditional cost effective teaching based on the voice and skilled use of chalk'.

Your taxi driver can put the boot in if a hatchet job is required. Avoid HMI language such as, 'The staff might like to consider...' or 'In one lesson pupil participation might have been greater'. Settle instead for, 'That Mr Jones is bleeding crap, if you ask me', or 'The headmaster is about as useful as a porcupine in a jock strap'.

Finally remember that inspection is now a business, not a profession. Charge for everything — £100 extra for each piece of added vitriol, £500 for letting a duff teacher off lightly, and £1,000 for champers to celebrate with when you count the loot. Inspecting a school? Who needs 152 years of HMI tradition? Clarkie's right. Anyone can do it once he's read the manual. It's a breeze, guv.

Times Educational Supplement 1.11.91

In a right-wing land, Arbut is king

The right-wing now has an almost complete stranglehold on the education system. Little by little, vacancy by vacancy, Bill by Bill, the Right has occasionally slid, often raced, into an unchallenged position of power and influence. That it should have captured control by protesting over the imagined potency of an 'educational establishment' consisting of teachers, academics, inspectors and civil servants, is but one of a host of ironies and paradoxes that surround this astonishing phenomenon. Its ultimate vision not too far away now is 26,000 isolated schools or 'businesses', no HM Inspectorate no teacher-training institutions no local authorities, no unions preferably. Just the Government and 26,000 small businesses. A chilling re-creation of the 19th century.

Consider the history of the remarkable set of events of the past few years. Before the mid 1980s any proposals to treat education as a street market with children as cans of own-brand beans were seen as the gigglesome fantasies of an eccentric fringe. Today they are, following the 1988 Education Act, supreme orthodoxy.

Would anyone have forecast that the people chairing the two major national committees responsible for examinations and curriculum would be removed, and that both their replacements would be from the Number 10 Policy Unit? Or that vacancies on important national committees would unashamedly be filled with people who have not *an* ideology, but *the* ideology? I wonder if Kenneth Clarke rings up John Major, or more likely the other way round, and says, as in the BT advert. 'He's got an Ology'.

Many years ago I knew a man called Arbut, at least, that was his nickname. He was one of the great spotters of paradoxes, ironies, inconsistencies and inaccuracies, and his nickname derived from the habit of saying, 'Ah, but' at the beginning of his observations. Ever since then I have thought of an Arbut as either a unit of measurement of such inconsistencies, or a marker of them. He would have been in his element today.

Most recent legislation has come from ideas produced by right-wing pressure groups. Arbut, is it not the case that these were usually pretty flimsy, ill-researched, often conceived by people without appropriate firsthand experience of classrooms? Schools, it was said, would be liberated from government bureaucracy. Arbut, have they not been buried under vastly more control, form-filling and prescription about curriculum and testing than at any time in our history? A free competitive market would operate between different types of school. Arbut, did not the Government give millions of pounds extra to city technology colleges and grant-maintained schools?

The best Arbuts recently have been in teacher training and the New Zealand-inspired reading recovery scheme.

Kenneth Clarke has proposed that 80 per cent of teacher-training should be based in schools. Arbut, did not a research report by Warwick University show that teachers were already overwhelmed by government demands and were only able to spend a third of their very long working week in the classroom?

Undergraduate BEd training courses should be reduced to three years, analogous to his desire to have two-year university degrees. Arbut, is not the probationary year about to be abolished and would this not, therefore, reduce a five-year induction phase to just three, putting the profession back to the Fifties and the two-year certificate course, given that the third year would be spent in schools? Does this not come at a time when European countries are strengthening links with higher education, complaining about the shortness of British courses, and when we ourselves are basing nurse training more firmly in higher education, rather than leaving nurses to pick things up on the wards?

I found the announcement about the £3 million for the New Zealand reading scheme hilariously ironic. It was exactly 20 years ago that I had a grant from the Nuffield Foundation for a remedial language programme. We gave more than 100 five-year olds, in what was then called a social priority school, the English Picture Vocabulary Test and asked each teacher to rate language proficiency on a five-point scale. The lowest achieving quarter was split into experimental and control groups. Each child in the experimental group had individual attention, designed to suit his or her own language needs, for 45 minutes every day from an experienced deputy head given leave for the project.

We delayed six months before following up with tests, to avoid Hawthorne Effect from the excitement of an experiment, but the experimental group won hands down and was, on average two clear

Ladybird readers ahead of the control group. Arbut, was not compensatory education widespread in the 1970s, did not the New Zealand team draw inspiration from good work in Britain and the US, and are they not (wash your mouth out with soap and water) *academics*! Were not both remedial work and teacher release badly damaged by the very cuts in government spending advocated by the right-wing?

Kenneth Clarke is now recruiting a fresh team of advisers, so should you wish to receive at invitation to advise the Government about education, I have obtained from him the six tough new requirements, or 'performance criteria', you will have to meet. You must be able to answer, hand on heart, Yes' to *all* the statements below:

- ☐ I am very, very, very right-wing;
- ☐ I have not been inside a classroom for years and have no teaching experience;
- ☐ I think all teachers, academics, inspectors and civil servants are raving Marxists;
- ☐ I am very, very, very silly;
- ☐ I can write really silly pamphlets that will have you in absolute tucks before you turn them into legal requirements;
- ☐ I can rotate one eyeball clockwise and the other anti-clockwise at the same time.

Some of these used to be optional, but they are in future compulsory. If you can answer a truthful 'Yes' to all six, please send a stamped addressed teacher to: Kenneth Clarke, c/o John Major, 'Arbut', Biggotts Welcome, Dunsmilin, Cossit. Herts.

Times Educational Supplement 24.1.92

An easy scapegoat for Clarke's propaganda

When Kenneth Clarke announced in January that 80 per cent of the one-year Postgraduate Certificate in Education (PGCE) course would be school-based, that was only the tip of a very large iceberg for teacher training. He also said he wanted the four year BEd course, the other route of entry into teaching, reduced to three years.

Mr Clarke's speech was predictable. An ambitious Minister, tipped as a possible future Prime Minister (but then, so was Kenneth Baker, so I take heart), comes into education from the heady reforms to the National Health Service, and finds nearly everything turned over. Teacher training offered a convenient scapegoat for real or imagined ills.

A great deal of school-based teacher training goes on now, and teacher trainers are committed to it. Mr Clarke perpetuates misinformation from right-wing groups, such as the Centre for Policy Studies, which claims teacher training consists of history and philosophy lectures from Marxists eager to brainwash trainees.

A recent survey has shown that 50 per cent of the PGCE course is already school-based, and it would be hard to find any history lectures or Marxism. PGCE courses teach 'theory' in a thematic way, covering topics like children's learning, the national curriculum, home and school, special educational needs, class management, specialist subject teaching methods and other unrevolutionary topics. Also school experience provides valuable links between theory and practice. Evaluations of 'on-the-job' training schemes show trainees wanting more such practical 'theory', not less.

If Mr Clarke's ill thought-out proposals go through, there is no doubt that the consequences will be severe. Trainees would only have the equivalent of 35 days in a training institution. They would spend the vast majority of their time in front of a class, copying one kind of practice, bereft of much more than a stick of chalk, what common sense they can muster and occasional help from a busy teacher. A study by Warwick University showed that teachers are drowning under the demands of local management, the national curriculum and testing, and only spend a third of their week teaching. Her Majesty's Inspectorate's report on school-based training stressed that teachers' main duty was to teach children, not train teachers.

The proposal to base training in a relatively small number of 'lead schools' is flawed. It cuts out numerous schools which might have particular departments, say maths and science, which are models of good practice. Even sillier is the intention that lead schools should be selected according to 'performance criteria', such as high exam scores and low truancy rates, and should include independent schools. Learning to teach without facing truancy problems or struggling pupils, would be like learning to drive on a disused airfield and then heading for central London.

Most other European countries want to strengthen the links between higher education and teacher training, not weaken them. Even in Britain the Government that proposes to distance the teaching profession from higher education is trying to bring nursing closer to it, on the grounds that learning on the wards is too superficial.

For some of our best known university schools of education, the financial consequences of Mr Clarke's proposal to remove what he called a 'considerable' amount of their money would be severe. Those that do mainly secondary PGCE work could lose most of their funds. If they close, their research and development work, their in-service and their higher degrees for serving teachers, which usually involve them in school-based projects, will be lost.

Contrary to Mr Clarke's propaganda, most tutors in schools of education have their feet firmly on the ground and have been involved in many national curriculum development and evaluation initiatives. They also have to teach regularly in schools. Much work on professional skills is based in universities, and the New Zealand remedial reading research by Professor Marie Clay, currently favoured by our Government, was initiated in Britain in the Sixties. HMI reports on university schools of education congratulated them on their good initial training, in-service work and research.

The likely proposals for primary training and for BEd courses are even more worrying. Primary teachers are overwhelmed by the demands of the national curriculum in nine different subjects, and readily admit they lack the subject knowledge to train students in fields like science and technology. At Exeter University we have trainers with PhD degrees in science and successful primary experience. Mr Clarke's three-year BEd degree plan and the Government's wish to see BA and

BSc degrees reduced to two years arouse scorn and incredulity from our European partners, already dismayed at the brevity of British training programmes.

The pity is that Mr Clarke decided to rubbish teacher trainers and caricature PGCE courses, hardly surprising since he has only visited one training institution, where students were astonished at his ignorance. Sadly, the Government's contempt for training has resulted in a proposal so ill-conceived it is a chilling re-creation of the non-training of the nineteenth century.

Observer 2.2.92

I'M A LICENSED TEACHER, WE NEVER DID CALCULATORS

Nightmare on LMS street

Well, ladies and gentlemen, as I explained in my memo to you, I've brought together the whole of the senior and middle management team to try to resolve the desperate staffing crisis we face from next September, the like of which I cannot remember since I became head here 15 years ago. You don't need me to remind you that we have lost six members of staff, and because we are one of the most unfortunate schools in Swineshire under local management of schools, we can only afford to make one appointment. Yes, Mrs Jackson.

May I point out, headmaster, that we in the maths department have been carrying a vacancy for a whole year, and that we would have appointed someone last Christmas, if there had been a suitable candidate, so I think maths has to be top priority.

I quite agree, Mrs Jackson, but we only had one applicant. You will recall he was that chap with the third-class BEd in main PE and subsidiary loft insulation from Lyme Regis Polytechnic, who said in his application that he would only take the job if it didn't involve anything beyond tens and units. In any case, I think other heads of departments may well have an equally strong argument. Yes, Mr Harrison.

I don't see headmaster, how you can possibly ignore the case of modern languages. We've got the new national curriculum requirements coming on stream this September and at your request we're trying to diversify into more EC languages. In fact it was you who insisted that Mr Origamo should teach Italian, just because he has a foreign name and once worked in a Cornetto factory, even though he's only one lesson ahead of the pupils in our coursebook Bluff Your Way Round Pizzaland.

I do sympathise, Mr Harrison, but I can see that Mrs Bishop wants to put the case for science.

I certainly do, headmaster. We're absolutely desperate in science. There are so many pupils in each class because of staff shortages, we're having to do the whole GCSE syllabus with yoghourt pots, there's no room for any equipment.

We've got a biologist who doesn't know any physics or chemistry, and a physicist teaching A-level biology who couldn't tell a gastropod from a gas mask, or his artery from his elbow.

Look, I can see we could go on all day about everybody's bid, let me bring in Mrs Goodwin as deputy responsible for curriculum and staffing.

I think several departments have a very strong case, headmaster, and we need people to take PE, including school teams, especially football. Then there are art and music, and the humanities, English are a teacher short, and we've been asked to make our curriculum more multicultural. Technology could do with a new appointment as there's all this design and microelectronics stuff, and HMI have complained that Mr Peterson still insists everyone has to make a string cutter, because that's what he always used to do in woodwork.

Well look, ladies and gentlemen. I think we could spend weeks trying to resolve all these problems. The governors also want their say, though I'm afraid Mr Dubbins, the chairman, doesn't really understand our problems. Since we're strapped for cash, we can't even be sure of the grade or whether there's much of a future for anybody we appoint. So I tell you what. Leave me to draft the advert. I'll see what I can do to meet people's wishes. I'll sent round a copy of the advert to everybody for comments, and then I'll fax it off to *The Times Ed*, if our fax isn't still on the blink. I think that's the best we can do in the circumstances.

SWINESHIRE

SWINESVILLE HIGH SCHOOL

(School motto: 'Don't let the bastards grind you down')

Tel: Cut off
Fax: on the blink
Headmaster: Mr N. I. L. Desperandum

Required for September 1992 a versatile and enthusiastic **teacher of maths, modern languages, science, humanities, creative arts, English and, oh yes I nearly forgot, technology as well** on Standard Scale, or Incentive 'A' Allowance, depending on the outcome of the PTA's car boot sale and the £100 riding on Kemptown Boy to win the 2.30 at Cheltenham.

This exciting replacement (of six teachers at the last count) post will appeal to someone who relishes a challenge and who is gregarious, enjoying the company of large groups (say 40-ish) of young people each lesson. The postholder will join a team of colleagues who are closely knit, or 'nit', depending on the last head inspection, determined to implement the national curriculum if it kills them, as indeed it did in the case of the six teachers being replaced.

Someone bringing a multicultural dimension to the school would be welcome, but frankly we would take a Chukchi Eskimo if he or she could mend the bloody fax machine. As a result of the generosity of the governors a relocation package is available. It is box-shaped, and more commonly referred to as a tea chest. Removal expenses may be payable, but preference will be given to hitchhikers with big biceps.

Apply in writing to the headteacher, or in words of one syllable to Mr Harry Dubbins, chairman of governors, giving the names of a referee and two linesmen.

Swineshire is an equal opportunity employer. The opportunity of being unemployed this time next year is roughly equal, whichever school you teach in.

Times Educational Supplement 20.3.92

Trust me, I'm a certified plonker

It was a bit of a blow, psychologically speaking, to arrive at work the other day and find the place awash with signs saying 'Age Concern'. For one awful moment I thought my nightmare had finally come true and that, with three out of five members of the teaching profession now over 40, Age Concern had finally become our major trade union. It turned out they were merely having a conference in our building.

It had been quite a week for the Oldies, as a couple of days previously I heard someone say that being a school governor was now so onerous, no one with a family to look after or a full-time post could possibly manage to do it properly. What with a number of heads currently expressing their unease at the powers that their governors exercise, it did look as if it was about time that the partnership between lay and professional people in education should be thoroughly reviewed.

Few would deny that there is a proper place in education for lay people. After all, education costs billions of pounds of public money, eight million children and numerous adults are dependent on it for their personal development, and professional people might become arrogant if left entirely alone. What is astonishing is that so many thousands of school governors, some with numerous other commitments, are willing to give up time to attend what can occasionally be unutterably tedious meetings. Either we are exceedingly fortunate in the high degree of public participation in school governance, or the nation has more incurable masochists than is realised.

It is rather sad, therefore, that when so much has gone well, there seems to be growing disquiet at the things that are going badly. The main concerns are about governing bodies who are not able to discern that fine line separating genuine interest from undue interference, and so overstep it too frequently by trying to take on the day-to-day running of the school. Problems can arise, too, with individuals who dominate the rest with their own or their political party's ideology. Worst of all is when the chair of the governing body is the biggest culprit.

It would be a pity if the crass behaviour of a few led to a backlash against the valuable role played by the many. I well remember one head complaining bitterly about the malevolence of his school's governing body, when in fact there was just one complete idiot and one apprentice idiot. I realised he could not stand the complete idiot, because he was always thanking him profusely for his wise counsel, when everyone knew that more sense could have been obtained from a geranium. Silence would have said it all.

Perhaps what we need is a decent *Plonkers' Guide* which would spell out so clearly what the lay person should not do, that problems would never arise. I offer the following modest snippets for such a tome.

The seasoned plonker will volunteer to chair the governing body and then spend two hours on some piddling matter arising from the minutes of the last meeting. This will ensure either that the rest of the agenda has to be galloped through in record time, or that another meeting has to be arranged. It is also handy not to have read the papers beforehand and then to read them out loud as the meeting progresses. Educational standards being what they are in Britain it is safest to assume that no one in the room ever got beyond Beacon Reader 2.

Black-belt plonkers come into their own on appointing committees. A few unshakeable prejudices are always useful. Those struggling to find one or two of these could try exercising a veto against candidates with beards, anyone who ever taught in the Inner London Education Authority, or applicants who attended a poly. After the decision has been made, insist on debriefing the unsuccessful candidates yourself, preferably telling a couple that the committee did not think much of their alma mater, and the rest that their references let them down. This should ensure a steady stream of letters from vice chancellors, tutors, college principals and referees, and with luck the odd libel action.

One of the most effective ways of scuppering the school is to insist on trying to run it on your own. Feign knowledge about every aspect of the building trade, even if you are incapable of assembling a deck chair, and make out you are a financial wizard, omitting to mention that you could not tell a spreadsheet from an army blanket. At the first sign of misbehaviour demand that all miscreants be excluded from school, teachers always appreciate smaller classes. Fixing the salary of the head can also be enormous fun.

Always claim to be speaking on behalf of all the parents, even if you haven't the foggiest idea what they believe, and profess a close first-hand knowledge of the business community, especially if all this means is that you occasionally frequent the local chip shop. When it comes to the annual meeting of parents make sure you volunteer to address them at enormous length, as this can cut down the time available for trouble-makers to raise points with you.

Finally make sure that you always take the one place available to the governing body at any training courses, lest anyone else should have the temerity to go, but oppose any release of teachers for in-service, on the grounds that they should know how to teach already without having to go on a course. Whatever you do, never read a book or ask the head or a teacher for advice, as this could jeopardise your amateur status and be a serious obstacle to obtaining your full Plonker's Badge. Oh, and once you've obtained the full badge, order the head to take you on to the staff as a licensed teacher.

Times Educational Supplement 17.4.92

Forward to the bad old days

I made a big decision the other day. I decided I was going to do something really radical. It's all very well you cracking up laughing, but I am fed up of reading about the Government's 'radical' education reforms. Wandsworth's 'radical' plan to bring back selection at 11, or Mr Major's 'radical' views on GCSE coursework. It cannot be too long before my own kids start saying, 'When are you going to do something radical, dad, like the Government does?'

In my innocence I had always assumed that the way to be radical was to develop a dramatically different initiative that was well ahead of its time, but I now realise that it is nothing of the sort. These days to be radical is to be willing to go back in time to what was soundly rejected years ago, in the well known split infinitive of Star Trek command: 'To boldly go where lots of men have been before.' So cautious radicals merely reinstate something that was chuckled at in the 1950s, wild radicals reclaim ideas that drew guffaws in Edwardian times, and ultra-radicals look for practices that got belly laughs from the Tudors and Stuarts.

My radical idea is to go the whole hog, round up a class of children, take them to a deep cave in the South of France and paint a few bison and sabre-tooth tigers on the walls. I shall call it the Really Really Radical Palaeolithic Curriculum. The Centre for Policy Studies will be pig sick with envy.

It is questionable whether this whole educational time travel, back through the nostalgic veil of mist to Victorian England, will cease now that we have new ministers. I await eagerly a ministerial speech on education which mirrors exactly the one made by Virginia Bottomley to the nurses, when she said that what we desperately needed was a period of stability (loud cheers and applause), so the Government's reform programme would proceed as planned (chorus of groans).

Take the business of opting out. One way or another the Government is determined to see most schools opted out by the next election. So some schools opt out to claim the building bounty before the Treasury closes that one down, others talk of opting out to escape closure or redesignation as a selective school. Yet others are so short of cash that any avenue which appears to offer more loot seems attractive. Some schools want to opt out *en bloc* so that they can opt in again, and even small schools are being urged to opt out as a cluster.

But what kind of mad rationale is this? No one talks about what grant-maintained schools would be opting into, only what they are pulling out of. What they are opting into is the status of being one manila folder among thousands in some remote government bureaucracy that has not the foggiest idea of how to run individual schools.

We have already seen the sad spectacle, when things have gone wrong in a grant-maintained school, of ministers simply wringing their hands looking bereft, or putting Eric Bolton, former Chief HMI, on the governing body. Splendid chap though he is, I cannot see him making it to the 26,000 governors' meetings each term.

Governments can only take crude decisions about individual schools, like close them down. Since the Government has been trying to shut small schools for years, advising these to become grant-maintained and throw themselves on the mercy of a bureaucracy situated miles away in the capital city, would be like advising Little Red Riding Hood to opt out of Grandma.

Now that Kenneth Clarke has made his way off to the Home Office, no doubt saying to himself, 'I've learned my lesson. No more Mr Nice Guy', everyone hopes that the climate of complete contempt for the expertise of the teachers, teacher trainers, inspectors or local authorities, will have gone with him. The real test of the new ministers will be whether they can shed the pressures and prejudices of the hard right-wing groups who dominated two of the last three ministers, only John MacGregor being man enough to remain immune. Since they have the ear of John Major I suspect they will triumph again.

The new minister, having been at the Home Office, is said to be concerned about truancy. He will no doubt be interested in the scheme being tried out in one local authority. All heads have been written to and told to change their registration procedures. No fewer than 12 different letters are to be used in the case of absence, with W for 'out on work experience', N for 'sickness note', V for 'educational visit', C for 'circumstances like attending a funeral', and so on. No doubt category C will soon have appeared so often that, if they were all true, the whole county would be extinct.

Why stop at a mere 12 capital letters, however? With only 12 there is a sporting chance that the morning's teaching could commence as early as 11am. Anyone with a fertile mind wanting to occupy the whole day on registration could no doubt come up with even more, like S for 'Shop-lifting', M for 'more sense', F for 'fed up of tests' or B for 'bugger this for a lark'. Perhaps there could be multiple responses when there are several reasons for absence, and really skilful registration experts could eventually come up with BUNKED OFF.

One head I know claims he is not at all worried that truancy will affect his or his colleagues' pay packets. He argues that if absentees are out shop-lifting, then, given that they may well go on to become seasoned villains, this could legitimately be put down as W for work experience. If the indiscriminate chaos of 19th-century schooling, out of local control, scattered aimlessly across the nation, good for the few, poor for the mass, is to reappear in all its glory, then so perhaps will Fagin.

Times Educational Supplement 15.5.92

That crazy circular in full...

DFE CIRCULAR 5/92
The Education (Individual Pupils' Achievements, School Records and School Curriculum) (Amendment) Regulations 1992

The Department wrote to all primary and secondary schools on January 10 enclosing a copy of the Parent's Charter proposals. Document 1 dealt with annual pupil reports to parents. After careful consideration of the responses, the Secretary of State has now made the revised regulations given below to govern the reports which all maintained schools must send to parents on their children's progress in 1992. These Regulations are statutory obligations and must be obeyed.

I Duties and powers of headteachers
From the summer term 1992, headteachers *must:*

☐ ensure that a written report is sent to all parents;

☐ include in each report the minimum information required by the regulations below;

☐ stop whingeing about all the bureaucracy they have to deal with nowadays and how it wasn't like this in the old days when they first came into the profession;

☐ genuflect when passing the photograph of the Prime Minister and citizen's friend, to be installed in all school entrance halls from September

Headteachers *may:*

☐ exclude from the report information which could confuse parents (ie, most of it);

☐ shred thousands of copies of the school report form they have just squandered most of their LMS money on, as these are now totally useless;

☐ have a nervous breakdown (weekends only);

☐ translate the report into Sanskrit or Old Norse (not for any particular purpose, you understand just to keep them out of mischief).

II Minimum mandatory content

The regulations specify the minimum content of all reports. From the summer term 1992, all school reports *must contain:*

☐ **'brief particulars' of the pupil's achievements in each subject.**
'Brief particulars' means a short narrative commentary on strengths and weaknesses, and 'subject' means none of this topic and project crap from you people in primary schools

☐ **the name of the caretaker's dog.**
'Spot', 'Kenneth Clarke' (Rottweilers only), that sort of thing.

☐ **a summary of the pupil's attendance record during the year.**
Sarcastic comments like 'Who's he?' should be avoided.

☐ **the level of attainment on the 1-10 scale by profile component and subject.**
Teachers not sure what profile components are should write for an explanation to: I M Knackered, DES, Search Me, Utter, Berks.

☐ **where requested by parents, the pupil's level 1-10 by attainment target.**
Where pupils have been assessed at the end of a key stage, head-teachers are under a legal duty to respond within 15 days, to any parent wanting to know attainment target levels. The actual grades must be given, and the reply 'Stuff you, sunshine' can only be sent if the parent is known to have voted against opting out.

☐ **the deputy head's shoe size...**
or waist measurement. Is he/she a real smartass who needs humiliating?

☐ **comparative information about the levels of attainment of other pupils.**
The following codes must be used: BC = Bloody clever, would have passed the 11-plus, and will soon have to.
C = Clever, worth poaching by an aspiring city technology college.
A = Thick, but his parents think he's smart.
BT = Bloody thick, likely to be turned down by schools worrying about league table places, worth paying prep school fees to get him off the books.

☐ **the IQ of the chairman of the governors...**
to the nearest millimetre.

☐ **a list of all the kings and queens of England...**
Nothing to do with the pupil, but will please the right-wing pressure groups.

☐ **a complete set of national curriculum documents.**
Why should teachers be the only ones to suffer?

☐ **as much padding as possible**
Add a chapter of *War and Peace,* anything to make the report look substantial.

III Questions and Answers

Q   What is the scope of the regulations?

A   They apply to all maintained schools, but not to the private sector, so there.

Q   Has anyone actually asked the questions in this section?

A   No, I made all the questions and answers up to fill out the circular.

Q   All right then, what's the capital of Bulgaria?

A   Er...

Q   So when are teachers supposed to find the time to do these huge reports?

A   Isn't it Budapest? No, wait, that's in Hungary, isn't it?

Q   What if we've already spent a lot of money printing this year's reports?

A   Tough toe-nails.

Q   So are we going to have more of this Citizen's Charter stuff?

A   Shut your mouth and carry on typing those name badges.

Q   Is this circular not the biggest load of bureaucratic bullshit ever conceived?

A   Got it in one squire.

Times Educational Supplement 29.5.92

School children need testing.
So do schools.
Have you the skills to be a school
inspector?

The Parent's Charter introduced a series of reforms to increase parents' rights, to provide them with more hard, factual information about the performance of their local schools and to encourage higher standards. At least that's the story we're putting round to justify killing off HM Inspectorate after 150 years, simply because we think they're wishy-washy liberals who have pointed out one leaking roof too many.

'Registered inspectors' is the euphemism we have dreamed up for the assortment of amateurs who will rampage round schools pretending they know what is going on and collecting large sums of public money for it. There will be a fee paid for each school inspected. This may range from £5,000 to £30,000, depending on whether the school wants you to give it a grade D or an A.

Once you have become a registered inspector, you can tender for school inspections and you will be expected to form a team of equally bewildered dilettantes to work with you. You will be given a five -hour, or, if you are in a bit of a rush, a five-minute training programme and you will soon be coining it.

If you are fed up with the Job Centre, have just come out of Strangeways, can't afford a TV satellite dish, tend to belch loudly after a meal or pick your nose, qualify for Alcoholics Anonymous, travelled to Sweden to watch England in the European Nations' Cup, cannot spell 'up', think SEAC is the capital of Albania, and have the IQ of a mentally subnormal gnat, then you could be just the person we are looking for. We **need** people who:

- know nothing about schools;

- have worked in some relevant job, like butchery;

- have tried pyramid selling and want a faster buck;
- think teachers are idle hippies.

We **do not need** people who :

- have taught in the classroom;
- believe inspection and advice go together;
- can tell an underachiever from an undertaker.

This is a flexible opportunity — once registered you can tender for as few or as many projects as you wish to take on. You could work nights, weekends, inspect five schools at the same time, stand in front of school assembly juggling chamber pots, make up your reports off the top of your head, write them in Latin, buy a new Porsche, split you sides with mirth at the dismay and anger of the staff. No one will give a toss, the cheques will be in the post anyway.

If you'd like more information about being a school inspector, please return the coupon below to: **Registered Inspectors, Rip-Off House, Easy Street, Mega, Bucks.** Or call us at **Post Restante, EI Dorado, Costa Packet, telephone number, Hawaii Five-O,** quoting reference 'Print Your Own Money'.

Times Educational Supplement 24.7.92

I know a cushy number when I see one ❏

I want loads of money *fast* ❏

I know bugger all about education ❏

NAME ————————————————————————

ADDRESS ————————————————————————

————————————————————————

It's Tee Hee Hee with the DFE

What they did in our holidays

For those who were away during that critical summer period, when the education system is put through the mincer in the safe knowledge that no one can do anything about it, here is a quick recap of what happened. The most significant event was the Government White Paper. This will set the scene for the next 25,000 years, the Secretary of State said, or maybe it was the next 2.5 years, or the next 0.25 years, I forget now. Anyway it sounded impressive at the time.

The central platform was opting out. Schools must in future legally adopt one of two titles which will appear on their headed note-paper. Names like 'comprehensive' or 'community' are now illegal. They can either call themselves Swinesville Been Really Sensible And Opted Out School, or Swinesville Complete Prat That Stayed With The LEA School. A new funding body is being established for grant-maintained schools, to be named the Loadsamoney Benevolent Society, and the Council for Local Education Authorities is to be reconstituted as the Oliver Twist Fellowship.

Small schools are being encouraged to opt out in clusters. Yet a safe distance away, in the very same White Paper, is a section on taking surplus school places out of the system, better known as 'closure' to ordinary folk like you and me. Nonetheless the Department for Education says it has already received several enquiries. One letter I saw read as follows: 'Dear Grandma, I am writing to say that I shall be opting out of your control in future. I'm sorry about this, but me and my friends met this really nice wolf in the forest the other day. Yours sincerely, Little Red Riding Hood.'

Another brilliant idea in the White Paper is the proposal to put the National Curriculum and the School Examinations and Assessment Council together in a single body, on the quite logical grounds that curriculum and assessment go together and should not be dealt with by two councils situated 200 miles away from each other. This is a stunning piece of inspiration, until you realise that they used to be under the same roof when the Schools Council existed. Then the Government decided, against all advice, that it would be a stroke of genius to take half the council away and send it up to York. Now they are to be reunited at huge expense. This cavalier attitude to public money and professional opinion will in the future be known in the literature as the Dick Turpin strategy.

Following its policy of putting a great diversity of people on national committees the government has continued to appoint people with very varied views to several important bodies. The National Committee for Castigating Teachers celebrated the appointment of Ronald Duck and Mrs Duck while Donald Ruck, and Mrs Ruck, Lord Muck and Lady Luck have been put on the newly formed National Council for Training Butchers to be School Inspectors.

The new style of school inspection was also made a little clearer during the summer. Apparently the main purpose of inspection, according to the DFE, will be to see how schools differ from the norm on performance indicators like truancy rates and test scores. I have immediately set up my own specialist school inspection company. We at Norm School Inspections Plc will concentrate entirely on inspecting schools that are average.

Our inspection will last precisely 25 seconds (or is it 2.5 seconds, or 0.25 seconds, I can't remember now, I'll have to ask the Secretary of State), and the conversation will go something like this: 'Hello, I see your truancy rates and test scores are at the norm. Goodbye.' We have already recruited our statutory butcher who will check out whether the school has the national average number of vegetarians, and will want to know why not, as well as how many lamb chops you would like next week.

The saddest spectacle of the summer, however, was the Great Annual Educational Paradox. This is a ritual observed every August when A-level and GCSE results come out. If the results are worse than previously, then it will be said that standards have gone down. If the results are better than the year before, then it will be said that standards have gone down. It is the only aspect of life where both 'up' and 'down' always mean 'down'.

What was different this year was the speed with which the Secretary of State rushed into the mass media to rubbish GCSE results in light of an HMI report no one had seen. In 1976-77 I was specialist adviser to a Parliamentary Select Committee that looked into the whole issue of examination results at 16. Our report was full of criticisms about lack of comparability between exam boards, between subjects and from one year to the next. The difference between then and now is that in 1977 nobody rubbished the exam itself, or the achievements of thousands of pupils and teachers who had worked hard for their O-levels.

So why, on this occasion, did the Secretary of State, on the basis of a report far less damning than our 1977 one on O-levels, cast doubts on the very nature of GCSE? Look carefully in future at the back of his jacket. Every morning when he puts on his jacket, he notices that the now all-powerful right-wing of his party (which wants to bring back O-levels and relegate the GCSE to the position once occupied by CSE) has taped a bullseye dead in the middle of the back of it. Every night when he gets home he removes 25 arrows, or maybe it is 250 or 2,500. If he wants to keep his job he has to play obedient dummy to these powerful unseen ventriloquists. Every Secretary of State nowadays should be called Archie Andrews.

Times Educational Supplement 18.9.92

Doctor, doctor, how my brain hurts

A few years ago I went to a particularly tedious and brain-corroding conference on the management of education. When it was over most of us headed gratefully to the railway station. On the platform, one delegate began to behave in a bizarre fashion, stepping first on to the train, then off it again, then standing poised with one leg in the air, near but not actually on the step into the carriage, with a blank and far-off look in his eyes. It occurred to me that the poor beggar must have become so disoriented by the sheer, numbing tedium of the conference that it had gnawed away at his brain.

Another time I came out of a meeting on performance indicators and asked a fellow member the way to the dining room. He replied 'Irra gorra imma there,' or something similar, and I realised it was exactly the same mental condition, except that in his case the power of coherent speech had been dissolved. I have since checked it all out in the medical literature, and the condition is officially known as *dementia managementia*.

The medical textbook define *dementia managementia* as 'a state of individual or collective mental deterioration, analogous to Mad Curriculum Disease but caused by excessive exposure to policy or mission statements, or to the defining, measuring or recording of performance indicators'. It is also known as Baker's Syndrome. Sufferers can be recognised by their unsteady gait, heavily pouched eyes and slurred utterance of largely meaningless phrases like 'deliver the curriculum'.

I have been eagerly studying its aetiology in education, where it has only been identified since 1988. Before that time the few known cases baffled doctors, but in the past four years the World Health Organisation has estimated that virtually all heads and over 95 per cent of teachers have contracted mild or severe *dementia managementia*.

Fortunately the disease is not a permanent condition and the cure is simple. All you have to do is stop babbling Bakerspeak and talk to a colleague about something important, such as why someone hasn't learned to read, how to deal with a difficult pupil, or a particularly nifty strategy you have found for explaining magnetism. Or you can even play a game of darts or bridge and you will feel better right away.

What is particularly worrying is the way in which *dementia managementia* has been spread deliberately in order to control education in general and teachers in particular. Waging mass psychological warfare against a whole profession is very easy if someone is determined enough.

Let us suppose you want to control public transport and the driving of buses. Nothing could be simpler. First of all the system in general must be destabilised, so you start by suggesting that many bus drivers are incompetent and that the public should be scandalized about this. The fact that most bus drivers are, in reality, extremely skilled and conscientious is neither here nor there, what is important is to create the impression in the public mind that lives are at risk.

This uncertainty can be fomented by several means. First make high-profile pronouncements at major conferences, phrasing these in such a way as to ensure huge coverage in mass circulation newspapers. Talk about rapidly falling standards of driving, dissatisfaction from passengers, the need for radical reform. Next establish pressure groups. About ten people will do. They must set up a dozen groups which sound innocent and earnest, such as the Campaign for Better Bus Driving, the Centre for Avoiding Death in a Double Decker, or the Institute for Traditional Driving and the Elimination of Drunken Bus Drivers of Whom there are Too Many.

These ten zealots must then write lots of pamphlets urging the rapid reform of bus driving and ensuring maximum exposure on television for the suggestion that there once was a golden age of bus driving, probably in the 19th century, which has been wrecked by trendy bus drivers and the bus-driving establishment.

Then it will be time to flood the bus driving world with lots of directives, preferably changed the moment they are about to be implemented. Demand mission statements, policy directives, institutional plans, and millions of detailed objectives, all of which must be rejected as inadequate or out-of-date in the light of the latest circular or piece of legislation on bus driving. That done, you will be home and dry. Bus drivers and supervisors will have become gibbering wrecks, many will seek early retirement, depot supervisors will either pack in, become cynics or toe the line, and 95 per cent of employees will have become victims of *dementia managementia*.

I wonder if this authoritarian and paper-driven approach to the management of education, or bus driving, has any chance of success. When I meet the entrepreneur or captain of industry who is admired for the thousands of forms he makes people fill in, or the rapidity with which he changes his plans, I might be impressed. In the meantime it seems the exact opposite of what is needed in a creative enterprise like education.

Indeed, I have just popped through the past in my time machine to see if creative genius made much use of all the paraphenalia. Back in Athens in 5BC, I asked Socrates for his performance indicators, but he said he was too busy teaching a promising lad called Plato.

Things were no better in 16th-century Rome when I popped in to see Michelangelo. I wanted to look at his institutional plan and mission statement, but he told me to bog off as he was busy. Busy? What a cheek! He has no time, apparently, to write a mission statement, but all the time in the world to paint the bloody ceiling. I bet he never got *dementia managementia*, the jammy beggar.

Times Educational Supplement 16.10.92

Recycling the bumf they peddle

A rather thick letter arrived in the post the other day. When I opened it I discovered that it was from a school where the children had made their own recycled paper by scrunging up paper they no longer needed. It had a few holes in it, but there is nothing unusual about that. Most of the documents in the morning mail have holes in them, especially those describing the Government's latest ideas on education.

It was only when I looked carefully at the faint traces of previous print from its former incarnation that I detected familiar bits of prose. With great ingenuity the school had actually recycled old national curriculum documents. I quite liked the old science version, but what a stroke of genius to take obsolete NCC papers and use them to implement the very curriculum that is now out of date.

You want to study the new science attainment target 'materials and their properties'? Well simply pulp all the papers describing the old attainment targets, and you'll soon find out that one of the great properties of paper is that you can turn it back into another version of itself, but this time write something more intelligent on it. It is the ultimate act of cannibalism, a unique mixture of ingenious opportunism, national curriculum coverage, parsimonious use of resources, and sheer occupational therapy, as teachers gleefully join pupils in shredding and squashing the very papers that have made their lives so difficult. It must be more satisfying than making your own wine.

In our new throwaway education culture, where the word 'permanent' now means 'lasted as long as a week', it is difficult to know what to do with the tons and tons of redundant paper. A more environmentally friendly School Examinations and Assessment Council would have sent all its literature out on ready-perforated tissue paper. The latest White Paper, which has an even higher Flush-Down-the-Toilet Factor than SEAC documents, and the lorry-loads of parents' charters and other glossy brochures, are part of a gigantic paper-driven publicity campaign by the Government that has seen the bill rise from £100 million in the late 1970s to more than £6 billion last year, according to a parliamentary answer quoted by the journal of the Secondary Heads Association, the most sickening statistic I have seen for a long time.

The main problem with the paperchase approach to education is that nobody reads it any more. Judging by some of the stuff coming out of the National Curriculum Council I suspect that even the NCC no longer reads its documents. It is a bit like going on holiday and forgetting to cancel the newspaper — you return home and find the hall full of print that is so out of date you know you will never get round to reading a single newspaper. It reminds me of a Kafka novel: 'One morning Josef K woke up after a restless night to find that he had been turned into a gigantic SAT pack.'

Recycling obsolete documents may be one solution, but there must be others. A 'What to do with stale government documents' competition is called for. Perhaps they could all be laid end to end, stretching out into space as far as Alpha Centauri four light years away. In keeping with the recycling notion, any keen teacher so minded could then get children to study the 'Earth and atmosphere' topic of the science national curriculum, by looking through a powerful telescope, combing space to see if they can find the original 1988 smiling, glistening, well-brilliantined Kenneth Baker, proudly clutching the pink national curriculum consultation paper.

Another possibility would be to store all redundant papers in a darkened room, which could be numbered 101. Badly behaved pupils, instead of being excluded or sent off to the cooler or sanctuary unit, could be made to sit there for hours reading them and making notes. Standards of behaviour would improve dramatically. A variation of this punitive theme would be to link it to appraisal. Forget performance indicators and all that glob about teaching quality. Teachers with a positive appraisal would receive a two-year exemption from reading any NCC or SEAC papers, and those with a poor appraisal would be sent to room 101. Standards of teaching would improve dramatically.

Kenneth Clarke's ruling that history stopped in the 1960s prevents the paper being used in history lessons, which would have been a further neat recycling idea, but technology lessons could benefit. Pupils would consider, under the heading 'appropriate use of materials', how they might build an environmentally friendly house out of government papers. There would be no problems about insulation, as the sheer density of most of them would keep out the cold. Nor would there be any need for central heating, since most papers have produced enormous amounts of their own hot air. Programmes of study are abbreviated to 'PoS' by the NCC, so all PoS could be kept under the bed where they belong.

In fact, recycling government papers could become the most imaginative cross-curricular theme around. In PE lessons pupils could leap over them, power lift them, use them as goal-posts. Counting, measuring and weighing them would knock off a few maths targets, and in RE they could pray that their volume and opaqueness will in future be reduced.

Music lessons could involve composing a song or opera, with SEAC documents as libretto. A Gilbert and Sullivan style might be most appropriate here. Finally they could write a poem about them, which would satisfy part of the English national curriculum.

> *I wander'd lonely as a cloud*
> *That floats on high o'er vales and hills.*
> *When all at once I saw a crowd,*
> *Of teachers, high on happy pills.*

Times Educational Supplement 30.10.92

How to win funds and influence people

The staff of a large primary school were feeling rather upset. Three times the post of deputy head had been advertised, three times interviews had been held, but no appointment had been made. They demanded a meeting with the chairman of governors to find out why. 'Because,' he told them, 'no candidate has given a satisfactory answer to our key question.' What, pray, was this crucial question? 'What would you do to raise more money for the school?' came the reply. The only answer they had received was about letting out the premises, and they had thought of that themselves.

It seemed a sad indicator of the recent switch in values in education, that what mattered most was not the candidates' ability to teach, look after the curriculum, liaise with parents, enjoy good relationships with staff of all kinds, but rather to raise extra loot. Anyone coming through the door proposing a smart covenanting scheme, some nifty investments, or even putting the lot on Kemptown Boy in the 2.30 at Haydock, might have landed a plum job. It was just as silly as the prejudice held by one daft governor a few years ago that the tallest candidate for a headship should get the job. Welcome aboard the England basketball team.

Recently I came across a humorous book written in the 1950s about how to get a headship. It was an even funnier read than it must have been at the time. As an anachronism it was in a class of its own. 'Be sure you impress the representative from the LEA' was one instruction, 'as he will be the key person when the decision is made.' I fell off my chair laughing. Nowadays, sadly, the LEA official is more likely to be the one cleaning the governors' shoes, or sitting there with a happy smile and far-off look in his eyes, thinking: 'Stuff your headship, I'm on the next plane to the Bahamas with my redundo pay when this lot's over.'

The book was full of obsolete advice about career paths, interview strategies, application forms and even the right dress to wear. If you want a deputy headship at the primary school I mentioned earlier, you could go in stark naked so long as you can quote stock market prices. A new book of advice is needed, in line with contemporary practice.

A decent career path today might include brief spells of experience as an illegal bookie's runner. This would offer a bit of modest financial expertise, physical fitness and stamina, and the ability to vault over fences when evading the police, which could be useful when escaping from an angry parent. It would also be handy when facing the local butcher on new-style HMI visits looking for the inevitable illegalities in the school curriculum and assembly. Other valuable experience might be in the second-hand car trade (spotting teachers who have been 'clocked', or those with insufficient tread on their elbow patches), or as Speaker of the House of Commons (dealing with unruly adolescents), shepherd (governors' meetings) and mortuary attendant (governors' meetings).

When it comes to interviews, smarming round the chairman of governors is probably the current equivalent of impressing LEA officials. One tip sometimes offered is to find out the interests of the key person and then profess great personal dedication to them by saying: 'What a coincidence! Growing geraniums is also a great passion of mine.' As a lad I found this a useful ploy down at the local bop, until I danced with a girl who worked in a chicken factory. 'What a coincidence! Slitting chicken's throats all day long is also a great passion of mine' somehow did not seem appropriate.

So far as dress is concerned tips can vary. Some candidates, uncertain whether to opt for the safe traditional or the fashionably progressive, settle for Doc Marten's flat brogues, Marks and Spencer flared jeans, or British Home Stores hippy beads. Interviewing panels frequently confuse dress with ideology, so the more mischievous interviewees can give the panel a nervous breakdown by wearing a flashy Hawaiian shirt and explaining how keen they are on phonics, or a tweed jacket and woolly pullover from Dunn's and describing their enthusiasm for a test boycott.

Spotting future heads can be quite good staffroom fun. Is it the teacher in the smart suit, the go-getting power dresser, the quiet conscientious one reading the *Financial Times* instead of *Exchange and Mart*, or the cheerful lunatic who greets every new mailing from the School Examinations and Assessment Council with hysterical uncontrolled laughter? Far from there being a field marshal's baton in every soldier's knapsack, some teachers have the equivalent of an organ donor card in their wallet which states: 'In the event of my ever being daft enough to apply for a senior post, please contact my next of kin and ask them to have me locked safely away until I have recovered.'

What cheers me about good heads is that they have remained merrily immune from the Government's attempts to pick them off as faceless chief executives, muttering Bakerspeak all day long and brandishing performance indicators under their colleagues' noses. Retaining courage, a sense of warm humanity and loyalty to the whole community, while running a school in difficult circumstances, is the hallmark of successful headship.

I recently watched a young physical education teacher trying to teach basketball in a large gym with a loud echo. As he struggled to make himself heard, largely because he allowed several of the pupils to bounce their basketballs as he spoke, thus producing a deafening echo, he would call out in hoarse desperation from time to time, much to the mirth of the pupils: Hang on to your balls.' For those in senior positions in our schools nowadays, it is both the best advice and the most helpful warning I have ever heard.

Times Educational Supplement 19.3.93

New inspectors ancient and modern

Have you met any new-style school inspectors yet? Ever since Kenneth Clarke announced that a butcher could inspect a school, the world has waited eagerly to see what these privatised inspectors would be like. Now the story can be told.

The good news is that Stewart Sutherland, the Senior Chief Inspector, is an intelligent and thoughtful man who will not allow himself to be pushed around by ministers. Also, many of the registered inspectors have considerable experience of schools. For a few more years we can capitalise on the fact that some early retired HMI and LEA inspectors have craft skills they are willing to carry on using after early retirement. One day this short-lived supply of ready-made experts will dry and then we are really in trouble.

Now for the bad news. First of all the one-week training programme, based in an expensive hotel, is all very well if one is dealing with people who have a strong background in the appraisal of what happens in classrooms, but would be scandalously inadequate for others. Sitting watching a videotape and then writing a lesson critique, valuable an exercise though it may be, is a poor substitute for the rigorous training needed by people unused to school inspection.

I was horrified to hear from one of the newly qualified registered inspectors that, having completed the one-week training programme to get his secondary inspector's badge, he would only need one further day to become a fully qualified primary inspector and another day to get his special educational needs licence. Just seven days and you can be a fully fledged inspector of anything .

Perhaps my memory is playing tricks, but I seem to recall having spent rather longer obtaining my Scout badges. The second-class badge was not obtained in a week, I can tell you. No sir, before we became fully badged porridge makers and tent-stake manufacturers we received much more rigorous preparation. Nor did we get our first-class badge after a further day or two. Chopping down trees and transmitting messages in fast semaphore or Morse code took rather longer. So the news that becoming a registered school inspector is about as searching a process as learning the Highway Code, and less so than qualifying as a first-aider, is very bad indeed.

Much worse, however, is the story on lay inspectors. At least the registered inspectors have a solid lifetime of prior professional experience, but the picture on the lay inspector front is utterly alarming. There may be a few of Kenneth Clarke's butchers, but the first noticeable feature of lay inspectors is that they are — well, not to put too fine a point on it, knocking on a bit, elderly, long in the tooth, matured, in the full bloom of life, antediluvian, superannuated, hoary, well past their first spring.

You know you are in trouble when people use words like 'sprightly' to describe you. Like 'strapping', it is a word which reveals more than it conceals. A rather more youthful person who attended a gathering of lay inspectors told me that the average age of those present was 63 if it was a day, but that some seemed sprightly, others inert. Most were retired males who had attended school themselves in the 1930s and were astonished to discover that some classrooms were no longer laid out in rows, that Latin had disappeared, and that teachers seemed very young. I suppose when you are older than all the teachers in the school you are inspecting, they do seem rather youthful.

One lay inspector, a sprightly man in his mid-seventies, wanted to join some national federation of lay school inspectors. Why bother? I would have thought a new specialist branch of Age Concern or Help the Aged would fill the bill. Why on earth are we recruiting an unsupported group of willing but elderly amateurs to undertake something as sensitive as appraising the quality of education? This is, after all, a programme of school inspection, not *The Antiques Roadshow*.

If you see the entrance to a school cluttered up with bathchairs, walking sticks and life support machines, then the lay inspectors are in town. No longer will teachers need to be told which lesson is being inspected, the unmistakable clunk clunk of an approaching Zimmer frame down the corridor will give ample notice, and when the poor beggar eventually reaches the lesson, it will be time for the bell.

Remember to tell pupils not to make loud or unexpected noises, as you don't want a heart attack on your hands. For those teaching Victorian social history it will be useful to have an authentic living artefact as a visual aid, complete with contemporary regalia, like an ear trumpet. At the end of the inspection lay inspectors may prefer to be paid in heating vouchers and Saga holiday tickets. One bonus is that free bus passes should keep down travelling costs.

Before anyone writes in to complain. let me say I know that out there somewhere is a vigorous 35year-old who bears no resemblance to the elderly stereotype. None-the-less, lay inspectors at present are predominantly male school governors of a certain (or uncertain) age. Far from being a Darby and Joan club, it is a Darby club, a ridiculous Dad's Army that should not be turned loose on an exercise formerly done by professional HMIs with more than 150 years of tradition behind them.

It is not their fault for volunteering to be active in their old age (that is entirely laudable), but rather the Government's for demeaning the teaching profession once more by pretending that teaching is a push-over, so anyone can inspect it. We shall all be 70 one day, but I hope no one encourages us to while away the hours by developing a fresh interest in scrutinising cantilever bridges or inspecting triple-by-pass surgery.

Times Educational Supplement 16.4.93

The polys are sitting pretty

In the autumn, Grimstown Polytechnic will become the Charles Chol-mondeley Marjoribanks University. It was going to be renamed the City University of Grimstown, but the director, now vice chancellor desig-nate, advised that it would be better to use the name of the millionaire ball-bearing manufacturer who had been such a munificent benefactor.

Second-year student Harry Ramsbottom, working-class, beer-swilling candidate for the BSc in Carburettor Tuning, will suddenly become suave wants-to-work-somewhere-in-the-City third-year wine connoisseur Harold de Vere Ramsey in the Porsche School of Auto-mobile Sciences.

That, at any rate, is the stereotype: the polytechnics acquire university status, move upmarket and jettison their horny-handed age. When the so-called 'binary line', which divided what used to be public-sector higher education, run by local authorities, from the élite charter-endowed university sector, is finally obliterated later this year, the true story will be somewhat different. The last group of similar recruits, the colleges of advanced technology, such as Bath and Bradford, that be-came universities in the 1960s, kept their flavour but also evolved their own distinctive style.

Years of sniffy inbuilt snobbery towards vocational education meant that British polytechnics, most created in 1966 (though Quintin Hogg had set up the Regent Street Polytechnic in 1880) never acquired the high status of the *technische hochschulen* in Germany. They were under-funded and often housed in appalling buildings. The second-class label was reinforced everywhere: they were not permitted to give their own degrees, but had to be validated either by their local university or by the Council for National Academic Awards. Her Majesty's Inspectorate moved freely in and out of their premises, whereas it was allowed to enter universities only by invitation, and then solely to look at teacher-training courses.

Some polytechnics have introduced shortened degrees, a move they may regret if they are permanently labelled the 'two-year degree' universities, especially as our three-year degrees already look slight in the new Europe where four years is commonplace.

Yet, despite the many constraints, they have broadened the base of higher education by recruiting more mature entrants and students from ethnic minorities, forged close links with employers and developed a wide range of flexible modular courses at both degree and sub-degree level.

Becoming a university will simply be one more evolutionary step. In recent years they have broken away from local authorities, been given more control over the granting of degrees, acquired their own funding council and admissions procedures, and increased research. From the autumn there will be a two-way process: they will have just as much effect on universities as universities have on them.

Government policy on higher education is quite simple nowadays. The central principle is 'Let's have more of it'. The method of implementing this objective is based on a crude market model, whereby student numbers are increased annually and higher education institutions bid competitively against one another for quotas of places. Instead of each institution being given an annual budget in blocks of five years at a time — the old quinquennial system of the 1960s and early 1970s — the Government, through the funding councils, puts student places up for auction.

Let us suppose that there are 1,000 fully funded places available in Necromancy. Each institution would send in its bid for a quota. The only advice available on what price to put on the head of each student in the bid is what is known as the 'guide price', roughly the average cost per student place in each subject, which for Necromancy might be £3,000. A particular university might decide to bid for 45 students, asking for 30 places at £3,000 and 15 at £2,800. The funding council then considers all bids and assigns 1,000 Necromancy places at different prices to different institutions.

In practice it is, from the Government's point of view, a neat voucher system without the vouchers. Money is attached to students, so institutions fall over each other to push up their numbers, often merely to pay off their growing overdrafts. Most have been willing to take additional students beyond their fully funded quotas, for the tuition fees alone, which may be less than half the 'guide price'. It is not surprising that, as buildings crumble, class sizes increase and staffing ratios worsen, university vice chancellors have asked for another £450 million to shore up their budgets. The Government would point out that, though the system may be crude, it has pushed up the participation rate in higher education from 14 per cent to 20 per cent, a significant move from an élite to a mass higher education system.

At present, polytechnics bid against each other with one funding council and universities hold their auction with another. From next year the two councils will merge — indeed, they have virtually done so already, and there will be a single Higher Education Funding Council located in Bristol. University vice chancellors are worried that a free-for-all competitive bidding system to a single funding council will drive down the money available per student place, the 'unit of resource' as it is known, to even lower levels.

The biggest change to affect universities will undoubtedly be the importing of some of the polytechnics' practices in auditing and rewarding teaching quality. Reports from Her Majesty's Inspectors play an important part when places are assigned through their funding council. If Grimstown Polytechnic wants 45 Necromancy students then the HMIs at the meeting which assigns places will be asked for their quality rating of the Grimstown course. They will consult their list and pronounce 'big Q', 'little Q' or 'no Q', depending on their private quality grading system, and this will be influential both on the number of student places granted and the amount of cash attached to them.

In the universities there is, as yet, no rating of quality in this formal manner. The Committee of Vice Chancellors and Principals sponsors its own teaching quality audit, but this tends to look at procedures for improving teaching, whereas HMIs actually sit in on classes to see whether lecturers communicate with students or merely mumble to the blackboard, the wall, or their shoelaces. There is no doubt that during the next five years some system of teaching quality audit that applies to both the existing and the new universities will have to be devised and that, in future, poor quality teaching will lead to a loss of income.

Universities are already used to differential funding based on quality rating, but only in research, and it is here that the polytechnics will have new tricks to learn. The first major appraisal exercise involving the newly expanded university sector has already begun. At the end of June all higher education institutions will send in their complete research records since the end of 1988. These submissions will be graded by expert panels in each subject and millions of pounds of research money will be handed out.

Some polytechnics already have a good research record and will do well, but many individual departments have done little or no research and will have to make the decision whether to earn their income entirely through teaching in future, or develop a research track record that will win them funding next time round. They will have to continue to be fast learners at the Charles Cholmondeley-Marjoribanks University.

Observer 7.6. 92

Seeds of destruction being sown in a three-class system

When Kenneth Clarke cleared his desk at the DES last month, packing his well-thumbed *Thesaurus of Insults*, he left his successor with numerous unresolved paradoxes.

Schools were supposed to be locally managed, yet it was the Government that was deciding every detail of the curriculum, the pupil testing programme, and the formula which determined how much cash they received. There had been a teacher shortage, yet teachers were being fired because schools could not afford them.

Standards were supposed to rise through competition between different types of schools, yet independent schools were free to teach whatever they liked, and maintained schools were told what to teach.

Opted-out schools and city technology colleges had been given millions of pounds for brand new buildings, while local authority schools endured leaking roofs and peeling paint.

One of the most puzzling paradoxes in this cash-dominated climate is the future of small schools. In many rural counties, small village schools with two, three or four teachers are commonplace. They know, more than any other sector of education, what a cash crisis means, for they have lived under the threat of extinction for years. Only the determination of local authorities to defy government edicts on closure has kept them alive.

Yet this very same Government is now trying to persuade them all to opt out of local authority control in clusters. It is clear that, once they have lost local authority subsidies, they cannot all survive. Ultimately, once the bounties have been withdrawn and they have been starved of cash, the weaker schools will have to close.

It is no surprise that teachers are left wondering what has happened to all those fine-sounding aspirations in official documents about 'developing the whole child' and 'a broad and balanced curriculum'. In this market-made world, the language of trade and commerce has come to dominate discussion about education. Children used to be 'taught', but in the cans-of-beans culture that permeates schooling nowadays, the curriculum is 'delivered' through 'delivery systems'.

Once the commercial analogy is accepted, everything else falls into place. The organisation must be lean to be profitable, so emphasis is placed on the delivery of a basic curriculum. The message is: put your effort entirely into what will be measured and displayed in the new league tables, to be introduced under the Citizen's Charter. Out-of-school activities, and subjects such as a second foreign language or classical studies — which are not in the national curriculum and will not be league-tabled — are regarded as 'frills', likely to siphon money from the profitable production of the basic model. If schools want to provide them, then the customer, in this case the parents, must be prepared to pay for them, runs the market argument.

This extraordinarily myopic view of education is not only an extreme form of philistinism, but constitutes a particularly shabby preparation for life in the twenty-first century. Alvin Toffler said that all education is a vision of the future, and that failure to have such a vision is a betrayal of the nation's youth. Children now in school will only be in their teens and twenties in 2000. Among the speculations for the future are that there will be increased leisure, that people may have to retrain many times in their jobs, and that, since multi-channel television is likely to spread to most homes, we will become a nation of passive spectators.

One significant insurance policy against a future in which citizens are totally dependent on the state and piped entertainment, is a broadly founded education which equips them to take control of their own lives. Shaving the curriculum back to a dreary diet of basics, treating course-work as second rate, starving schools of the cash for rich and varied extracurricular activities, and cutting back severely on youth and community education — something which numerous local authorities are forced to do to stay within budget — are all inimical to that vision of adult autonomy.

It does not take much imagination to see the Victorian three-class railway system which all this is producing. Many schools will feel driven to take the short-term cash premium which John Major admitted, in a letter to the National Union of Teachers last August, was being offered as an inducement to them to opt out of their local authorities. Independent schools will continue to provide whatever curriculum they choose, alongside a rich array of extra-curricular activities. The new, semi-independent sector of city technology colleges and opted-out schools will be given bounties to help them compete, but in the longer term will raise extra funds from their better-off parents.

This will leave a sector of the population, the least well-off and most needy, in cheap, cheerless third-class schools run by clapped-out and impoverished authorities, following a people's basic curriculum, set and tested by the Government. There will be no money for anything beyond it.

Every time vandalism, mass youth crime or joy riding breaks out, the finger is pointed at a lack of educational and recreational opportunities. If, in the twenty-first century, the narrowly-educated, socially-dependent masses occasionally leave their couches to create mayhem then no one should be surprised. The seeds are being sown now.

Observer 17.5.92

No solution to the sum of discontent

I cannot understand why there is all this fuss about some mathematician claiming to have drawn up a 200-page solution to Fernet's Last Theorem. I solved it about five years ago on the back of an envelope, no sweat. The newspapers have been full of inaccurate accounts about how this was a major breakthrough, the greatest mathematical triumph of the century and so on, but it is all baloney.

For those not in the know, here is the truth about Fernet's Last Theorem. It was claimed that no one had ever managed to prove that if you raise the amount of committee decision-making in education by any power beyond two, and then add to the number of prats influencing the Government, the result is a big mess.

I proved this conclusively years ago. Let the fact that the amount of committee decision-making has been raised be called c^r, and let the addition of prats advising ministers be a^p, then $c^r + a^p = $ crap.

Fernet must have worked in education himself. No wonder it was his last theorem. He probably shot himself after opening his final SAT pack.

The problem is that there is little decent co-ordinated advice being given to the Government and what bit there is gets ignored or distorted. Political advisers influence ministers, rather than Her Majesty's Inspectorate, once the trusted eyes and ears of the education service. HMI now consists of a few bedraggled survivors after the huge culling that has taken place since the decision was taken to privatise it. I rang up someone at the Department for Education recently and overheard a conversation among the telephonists: 'This chap wants Mr Farnes Barnes. Is he still here?'; 'I don't know, I think so. Give him a ring and see if he answers.'

What a brilliant communication system. So many inspectors have left, you just refer the caller to whoever answers the phone. 'Hello, it's the Minister here, I want to speak to the inspector responsible for infant schools.' 'Just a minute, I'll put you through.'

'Good morning, head floor-polisher here, how can I help you? Infant schools? No, you've got me there guv. 'Ere, have you thought of getting a few mums in to teach the little kids? Straight up, squire, could be a winner. Give 'em a few weeks training, no one would ever notice.'

Most of the few inspectors who remain are demoralised. They have seen their job changed from a highly esteemed profession with 153 years of tradition into something that a few dummies can supposedly be trained to do after a week in a hotel. I wonder if they use the same hotels over and over again. If so, they could recruit some of the staff who must have picked up a few tricks eavesdropping on the training sessions. 'Coffee, sir? Certainly. By the way, it's two r's in curriculum.'

Worst of all inspectors also have to act as Government snoops, filling in a proforma when they visit schools, reporting on whether or not schools are breaking the law (as many do if they are not teaching about the Aztecs or conducting their assembly in accordance with the rules), and who did and who did not boycott the national tests. This kind of petty crime logging should not be a job for expert education advisers. It is like asking surgeons to mend socks.

Why not just send PC Plod from the local nick instead? 'I was proceeding along Swinesville High Street your honour, when I happened to see a teacher failing to test her class of seven-year-olds on the building technology of the Pyramids and the Parthenon. When I apprehended the suspect she said, 'It's a fair cop. You've got me bang to rights. But you're not taking me alive, copper'. She then sat reading national curriculum documents until her head exploded.' Once the police have got league tables, performance-related pay and all the other market paraphernalia bequeathed by Kenneth Clarke, that sort of thing should move them right up the crime-busting league.

Even worse, HMI finds its reports are distorted by ministers to endorse their policies, while it is not able to speak out to denounce the fact. Ministers secure great publicity for their own version of what HMI has said by issuing a press statement before the report is widely available for checking. This gives them a huge advantage.

In this weird propaganda world, where white is black and black is white if ministers say so, John Patten was able to rubbish the GCSE last summer before anyone could see the relevant HMI report, and Baroness Blatch announced that the HMI report on the articled and licensed teacher scheme was a wonderful endorsement of Government policy. In fact it said the licensed teacher scheme was a shambles, only rescued by teachers' goodwill, and the articled teacher scheme, costing three times as much and lasting twice as long as the conventional training course, produced teachers who were not significantly different.

Exactly the same laundering will take place when HMI says what a scandal the Mums' Army idea has been.

Many schools are now understandably quite apprehensive about the new style of inspection, with programmed zombies coming armed with performance indicators, crime report sheets, blabbering newspeak and trying to hide their lay members. Fernet's Next-to-last Theorem probably stated that the amount of stress during new-style inspections is inversely proportional to the extent to which teachers can see the funny side of the whole tragedy. I like to think of a lay inspector watching one of those sex education lessons where the teacher stuffs a banana into a condom. Then I have hysterics imagining the local butcher trying to find the category 'teacher rams fruit into johnny' on his crib sheet.

Times Educational Supplement 9.7.93